A Guide to the Reformed Common Agricultural Policy

by

William Neville
of Burges Salmon

and

Francis Mordaunt
of David Anderson & Co

1993

Estates Gazette

A member of Reed Business Publishing

The Estates Gazette Limited
151 Wardour Street, London W1V 4BN

First published 1993
ISBN 0 7282 0189 5

Typesetting by Amy Boyle Word Processing, Rochester, Kent
Cover design based on an original painting by Graham Watts
Printed in Finland at Werner Söderström Osakeyhtiö

CONTENTS

A. INTRODUCTION

B. THE AGRIMONETARY SYSTEM

Paragraph 1.1   Introduction to the agrimonetary system

1.2   The new system

1.3   Effect on farmers' prices

1.4   Trigger points for green pound changes

    1.4.1   The final reference period

    1.4.2   Four-point gap between two currencies

    1.4.3   Six-point gap between two currencies

    1.4.4   Realignment

1.5   When green pound rate changes take effect

    1.5.1   Institutional prices

    1.5.2   Compensation payments

1.6   Switchover

    1.6.1   Correcting factor and reducing coefficient

    1.6.2   Marketing years

1.7   Possible protection against revaluation in floating currency Member States

C. ARABLE CROPS

2.   Introduction to arable crops

3.   The common organisation of markets

    3.1   Cereals

    3.2   Oil seeds

    3.3   Proteins

4.   An outline of the new system

5.   Area compensatory payments

5.1   Eligible land

5.2   Arable crops

    5.2.1   Cereals

    5.2.2   Proteins

    5.2.3   Oil seeds

    5.2.4   Linseed

    5.2.5   Vining peas

    5.2.6   Maize

F. INTEGRATED ADMINISTRATION AND CONTROL

G. A FINAL THOUGHT

Foreword

For many of us the intricacies of the pricing structure for agriculture have long been something of a mystery of the faith, confined to the "too difficult – esoteric – and obscure to comprehend" department. Most previously who had any claims to understanding the system acquired their knowledge piecemeal or even anecdotally with no comprehensive grounding in the basics of the systems which have held sway since we in the UK abandoned the Deficiency Payments System on entry into the Common Market in 1972 and espoused the Common Agricultural Policy (CAP) which formed such a central feature of the European Economic Community. For anybody involved with practical day-to-day working of farms and farming economics, whether in the sharp end as a farmer, or at one stage removed as a professional adviser, in one form or another, this has always been a very dangerous approach which frequently and devastatingly has found one out. Now, following the reforms of the CAP with the making of Council Regulation 1766/92, that approach to farming economics which was never sustainable, is exposed and a sharp learning curve has to be followed. No longer is the pricing structure concealed in the composition of market prices. Now, thanks to the restructuring, the EC's support to farmers is paid directly as a quasi grant, which represents the lion's share of the farmers entire reward. Farmers now "farm for the subsidy" and the rules for those subsidies have to be known and comprehended in every detail.

A number of commentators and MAFF itself have published explanatory memoranda of varying degrees of comprehensiveness, accuracy and sophistication. But until now nobody has attempted a truly in depth "Guide to the Reformed CAP". William Neville and Francis Mordaunt are to be congratulated and applauded for having remedied this yawning gap and omission so thoroughly with such a sophisticated analysis of this very difficult subject. Here we have not only a detailed commentary on the reforms of the arable sector with the area aid payments and new set-aside rules fully explained, but also the livestock sector with beef special premiums, suckler cow premiums and the sheep meat regime together with the very important and draconian enforcement measures and penalty provisions. Their work is truly a tour de force being right up to date in a rapidly changing economic climate while green pound devaluations suddenly convert forebodings of gloom into expectations of rewards for farmers at a level not seen in recent years.

Their task has been made more difficult by the fact that all the legislation is European with much of the substantive new rules contained in the recitals to the regulations which are couched in more generalised language than, for example, UK statutory instruments. Where UK domestic legislation is required to give effect to the EC Regulations, much of it is not yet available despite the fact that law as yet unacted has in some instances come into effect. In consequence, as with the evolution of milk quota legislation, a body of lore based on MAFF pronouncements or declaration of pious intent has built up and been transmogrified into law. To produce a commentary quickly when it is needed and before time has passed for a considered look at the new system is a daunting task.

This book is essential reading for anybody aspiring to advise farmers on any aspect of a professional service which requires consideration of farming economics including tax planning, succession for tenants or owner-occupiers, rent reviews, all aspects of the landlord and tenant system and all planning for owner-occupiers, rent reviews, all aspects of the landlord and tenant system and all planning for owner-occupiers or farmers operating other systems such as share farmers, farm partnerships, contractor agreements etc, conveyancers, accountants and all forms of financial adviser.

To have produced such a detailed and intelligible analysis of a very large area of new law in so short a time is a truly remarkable performance by the authors who are greatly to be commended for their efforts. *A Guide to the Reformed Common Agricultural Policy* must be prescribed reading for us all – agricultural consultants, land agents, agricultural valuers, solicitors, barristers, accountants and bankers as well as landowners and farmers. This work will appeal to those with a sophisticated knowledge and those with little or no prior knowledge of the structure of farm payments thanks to a short introduction and outline of the systems giving an overview before the reader is plunged into the interstices of the fine detail which has to be assimilated as only this book will now make possible.

Andrew Densham
Bristol
May 1993

Thank you

There are many people to whom Francis and I owe large thank yous for the help and encouragement received in writing this book. MAFF and SOAFD could not have been more helpful. However, one person's labours went so far beyond the call of duty that special thanks are due. She is my secretary Rose Jellie, who typed this book undaunted by the many adversities that beset us.

William Neville
May 1993

TABLE OF CASES

References in the main text are to paragraph number

TABLE OF EUROPEAN LEGISLATION

References in the main text are to paragraph number

Commission

PROPOSALS FOR REGULATIONS

NOTICES

TABLE OF STATUTES

References in the main text are to paragraph number

UK

TABLE OF STATUTORY INSTRUMENTS

References in the main text are to paragraph number

A. INTRODUCTION

Introduction

On May 21 1992, after four days of negotiation in Brussels, an unshaven and bedraggled Council of Ministers of Agriculture emerged rubbing their eyes, having finally agreed the first major reforms of the common agricultural policy in 30 years. These reforms affect cereals, oilseed and protein crops, beef and sheep. Whether they really knew what they had agreed to is doubtful.

Since then the Commission and member state civil servants have been busy enacting the reforms through Council and then Commission Regulations. In the UK we still await some of the statutory instruments that will give legal force to many of the announcements and demands from the UK's four agricultural departments.

The essential features of this round of reforms can be summarised under three main headings:

Supply control: Arable Set-Aside, Suckler Cow Quotas, Ewe Quotas

Price reduction: Oilseeds, Peas and Beans (to world market prices) Cereals and Beef (towards world market prices)

Compensation: Arable Area Payments (limited nationally/ regionally) Beef Headage Payments (limits imposed both individually and regionally)

The objectives of the reforms have been to control surpluses and in doing so reduce the cost of support to the European taxpayer, and at the same time satisfy some of the demands of the General Agreement on Tariffs and Trade (GATT). Reduced prices would, in theory, also benefit consumers, although to date the weakness of the pound sterling has cancelled out any potential savings for UK consumers. Finally, by giving farmers direct income aids, support would be targeting farmers rather than those engaged in handling and storing surpluses.

In order to make these reforms work two other ingredients were required. A reformed agrimonetary system, essential because of the advent of the Single Market on January 1 1993, and an Integrated Administration and Control System (IACS), required to ensure common application throughout the 12 member states and to prevent fraud. Following "Black Wednesday" in September 1992, when the pound sterling and lira fell out of the Exchange Rate Mechanism (ERM), the plans for agrimonetary reform had to be revised. Agricultural currency rates or "green" rates are still with us, and a series of green pound devaluations since September has meant that support prices have risen and that for farmers, at least, "Black Wednesday" has become "Golden Wednesday" – so far at least. The IACS legislation, on the other hand, has become the bugbear of the farming industry, setting up as it does a centralised bureaucracy to rival that now dismantled in Eastern Europe.

Whether we like it or not these reforms are likely to be here to stay, at least to the year 2000 and probably well beyond. This timescale fits in with the GATT Uruguay round which, if it is concluded, would be implemented over a six-year **period from** 1994. These reforms add to the already existing supply control mechanisms (milk, sugar) so that most of the major commodities are now covered. No doubt there will be continuing adjustments but the basic mechanisms are in place and will be used for the foreseeable future to bring the agricultural juggernaut under control.

For these reasons an understanding of the new basic mechanisms is essential for all those involved in the industry, whether farmers, their suppliers, the food industry or their professional advisers. Apart from the fact that farmers' incomes will now largely depend on following detailed rules and making extremely accurate returns, the reforms raise fundamental questions involving taxation, land and quota values and transfers, possible discrimination and landlord/tenant issues. This book sets out to explain the basic mechanisms and to explore some of the issues.

Inevitably parts of the book will be out of date before it is printed and the penalty of expressing views is that some will be shown to have been wrong. However, the book has concentrated on the main-frame legislation and central issues with a view to helping the reader work his way gently into this most complex subject.

B. THE AGRIMONETARY SYSTEM

Introduction to the agrimonetary system

1.1   Under the Common Agricultural Policy all farm prices, supports, rates of levy and compensation are expressed in European Currency Units (ECUs). In this way they are common to all 12 Member States. Under the old agrimonetary system they were then converted to national currencies by fixed agricultural exchange rates known as "green rates". These green rates were usually changed no more than once a year. A system of Monetary Compensatory Amounts (MCA's) was in place at border posts to iron out the trade distortions which the "fixed" green rates created as "real" currency rates fluctuated with the market.

Borders posts disappeared on January 1 1993 so that MCA's could no longer be implemented. The original Commission proposal on agrimonetary reform had been to abandon both MCA's and green rates and to revert to market rates, having had a once-and-for-all adjustment of support in ECU terms to prevent there being any winners or losers at the changeover date. All this was feasible without creating unworkable trade distortions so long as currencies stayed within the ERM. This plan was blown out of the water on September 16 1992 with the pound sterling and lira falling out of the ERM and becoming "floating" currencies.

1.2   The new system

A new agrimonetary system was drawn up and agreed by the Agricultural Council in December 1992 and came into force on January 1 1993.[1] Green rates have been retained and, for Member States with currencies outside the narrow band of the ERM (which includes the UK), the green rates shadow their market rates, never being allowed to move outside closely prescribed limits (basically 2%). In theory the green rate can be refixed several times in a month if market conditions determine. In this way they serve to avoid the trade distortions which MCA's were designed to prevent under the old system.

Green rates for Member States with currencies within the narrow band of the ERM remain aligned with their central rates and will change only after a realignment. The new system includes a provision for green rates used for converting export refunds and import levies set in ECUs to be fixed in advance for a period of up to four months.[2]

1.3   Effect on farmers' prices

The above is a simplistic explanation of the agrimonetary system which is far more complex for anyone needing to understand it on a daily basis. The important point for the farming industry is to understand that the new system will result in changes in prices and support on a

---

1   Council Regulation 3813/92 and Commission Regulation 3819/92 as amended.
2   Article 8 of Commission Regulation 3819/92.

much more frequent basis while sterling remains volatile against other European currencies and while other currencies are realigning. The table below shows the changes since September 1992 up to and including April 1 1993.

1 ECU =	Green pound changes £	% Change since Sept '92
Jan – Sept 1992	0.795423	–
Sept 1992 (2 devaluations)	0.818896	2.9
Nov 1992 (2 devaluations)	0.897524	12.8
Jan 1 1993	0.939052	18.0
Feb 1 1993	0.951031	19.5
Feb 3 1993	0.968391	21.7
March 1 1993	0.980715	23.3
April 1 1993 (no change)	0.980715	23.3

Between September and the advent of the new system there was a rise of 18% in institutional prices for UK farmers. Since January 1 and up to April 1 1993 there has been a further 5.3% rise, a total of 23.3% since September. The effect of this on the basic feed wheat/feed barley buying-in intervention price of 146 ECUs/tonne for the 1992/93 marketing year is a rise from £116.13/tonne to £143.18/tonne, a rise of £27/tonne.

The figures given in pounds sterling in this book are based on a UK green rate of £0.980715 = 1 ECU which was the rate applicable at March 1 1993.

Since mid March the pound sterling has strengthened against other currencies and, at the time of writing, a revaluation of the green pound (causing a fall in prices to farmers) is more likely than a devaluation.

1.4   Trigger points for green pound changes

1.4.1   The final reference period
Under the new agrimonetary arrangements, market exchange rates of currencies outside the narrow band of the ERM are monitored over three basic reference periods in a month, running from the first to the 10th, the 11th to the 20th and the 21st to the last day of the month.[1] If there is a monetary gap of more than 2% between the green rate and the market rate, averaged over the final reference period, the green rate is adjusted so as to halve the gap.[2] This mechanism triggered the changes on February 1 and March 1 1993. The monetary gap between the market rate for the pound over the final reference period in February 1993 and the green rate in force was -2.579%. This meant that the new green rate (effective from March 1 1993) reduced the gap between green rate and market rate to -1.29%.

Changes to the green rate of floating currencies can be triggered in other circumstances.[3]

---

1 Article 2 of Commission Regulation 3819/92.
2 Article 4 of Council Regulation 3813/92.
3 Article 4 of Council Regulation 3813/92.

1.4.2   Four-point gap between two currencies

When the percentage monetary gaps at the end of a basic reference period for any two floating currencies total more than 4%, then green rates must alter so that the total gap is reduced to 4% and each individual gap to not more than 2%.

1.4.3   Six-point gap between two currencies

In cases where a six-point gap develops between two floating currencies calculated over *three* consecutive working days, adjustments to the green rate will be made to any currencies which have opened up more than a 2% gap.[1]

1.4.4   Realignment

A monetary realignment within the ERM can trigger changes in floating currencies. Floating currencies must reduce any monetary gaps by half where they exceed 2% over an appropriate reference period. Such a realignment triggered the February 3 devaluation, when the Irish punt devalued by 10% against all members of the ERM.

1.5   When green pound rate changes take effect

1.5.1   Institutional prices

Another important point to grasp in the workings of the agrimonetary system is that changes to the green rates apply at differing times depending on the type of support. For institutional price support the effect is immediate and this applies to intervention prices (cereals, beef, butter, sugar) and other institutional prices such as milk target price, sheep basic price and sugar beet prices. Where payments to farmers are made over a period of time, it is a general rule that the most devalued green rate (ie the most advantageous to the farmer) should be used.

1.5.2   Compensation payments

For the new compensation payments the green rates to be used are those applying on the January 1 for the beef headage payments and on July 1 for the arable area payments.

1.6   Switchover

1.6.1   Correcting factor and reducing coefficient

The new agrimonetary agreement retains the so called "switchover" device,[2] which enables the strong currency countries to avoid reducing farm prices when their currencies are revalued inside the ERM. This is achieved by applying a correcting factor. In a year when the correcting factor is increased the institutional prices fixed in ECUs (not the new area or headage payments) are reduced at the beginning of the following

---

1   Article 2 of Commission Regulation 3819/92.
2   Article 9 of Council Regulation 3813/92.

marketing year by 25% of the change in the reducing factor[1] – the so called "reducing coefficient".

1.6.2 Marketing years

The following dates are the start of the marketing years for relevant UK commodities:

January 1	sheep basic price
April 1	milk, beef
July 1	cereals, sugar

At the time of writing there is uncertainty as to whether the Council will adopt the reducing coefficient for the price fixing for the 1993/94 year. If it does, prices fixed in ECUs will be reduced by just over 1% and the effect on July 1993 common wheat/feed barley intervention would be as follows:

July 1993 intervention   = 117 ECU/tonne
Divide by estimated reducing coefficient of 1.012674

Revised July 1993 intervention = 115.54 ECU/tonne
At current green pound rate   = £0.980715 to 1 ECU

                               = £113.31/tonne

1.7 Possible protection against revaluation in floating currency member states

There is provision in the agrimonetary legislation to allow floating currency countries to grant farmers compensatory aid when average green rates have been revalued in a 12-month period compared to the previous 12 months.[2]

This is optional in Member States and whether the UK would take up such an option if the pound strengthened in the second-half of 1993 is doubtful. However, this could be a useful safeguard in the event of a prolonged rise in the value of the pound.

---

1 Article 9 of Council Regulation 3813/92.
2 Article 8 of Council Regulation 3813/92.

C. ARABLE CROPS

Introduction to arable crops

2   One of the objectives of the common agricultural policy contained in Article 39 of the Treaty of Rome is to stabilise markets. By 1992 market balance in the Community was seriously adrift.

EC production and intervention stocks levels for cereals

Year	Total cereals production (million tonnes)	End of season intervention stocks (million tonnes)	Expenditure on export refunds[1] (million ECU)	Expenditure on intervention [1] (million (ECU)
1983/84[2]	123.66	11.34	988	351
1984/85	173.24	11.02	1,077	810
1985/86	160.53	16.56	1,712	1,347
1986/87	154.28	14.22	3,071	937
1987/88	153.96	12.06	2,925	1,275
1988/89	163.27	9.16	2,597	576
1989/90	162.29	11.80	2,267	948
1990/91	170.11	18.69	3,602	1,419
1991/92	181.03	26.32	3,140	2,497
1992/93	167.90	25.62	3,436	2,144

(1) From EC Commission's FEOGA Guarantee "Consommation de Credits" documents, based on FEOGA financial years.
(2) Does not include Spain and Portugal.
All figures for 1992/93 are provisional

The system of price support that has operated in the EC's common market in cereals set up by the Council since uniform support prices[1] has led to massive surpluses.

The system involves three prices for grain. These are the intervention price, the target price and the threshold price.

The intervention price is the price at which the community acts as buyer of last resort for grain of specified types and quality during limited parts of the year and in certain locations.

The target price is the level at which the community hopes producers will be able to sell within the community. Naturally it is set above the price offered by the buyer of last resort (intervention).

The threshold price is the lowest price at which cereals may be imported into the community. Import levies are imposed on grain imported into the community to cancel the difference between world and EC prices.

The three prices are fixed annually by the Council Ministers.

In 1986[2] a cereals co-responsibility levy was introduced aimed at making "producers more aware of the realities of the market" and in 1988 the ability to impose an additional co-responsibility of 3% of the

---

1 Council Regulation 120/67 replaced by Council Regulation 2727/75.
2 Council Regulation 2040/86.

intervention price of common wheat was imposed in conjunction with other budgetary stabilising measures, which resulted in cumulative cuts in intervention prices in all years save 1991/92.

In conjunction with co-responsibility levy additional co-responsibility levy and reduction in intervention prices the EC adopted set-aside and extensification schemes which Member States were left to implement. Despite this array of measures market balances were thought to be sufficiently bad to justify a new support system.

This was officially recognised in the recitals to Council Regulation 1766/92 stating that:

> The prices and guarantees represented by the machinery introduced by Council Regulation (EEC) No. 2727/75 ... encourage the growth of cereals production at a rate which is no longer in line with the absorbtion capacity of the market; whereas in order to avoid a succession of increasingly serious crises, the current policy should be radically reformed; whereas that implies that the support provided by the market organisation should be re-orientated in such a way that it no longer depends solely on guaranteed prices;[1]

By Article 26 of 1766/92 Council Regulation 2727/75 was repealed with effect from the 1993/94 marketing year.

---

1   First recital Council Regulation 1766/92.

The common organisation of markets

3.1　The common market in cereals[1]

Council Regulation 1766/92 sets up the common organisation of the market in cereals replacing Council Regulation 2727/75. It applies to all the obvious cereals such as wheat, durum wheat, rye, barley, oats, maize, grain sorghum, millet and canary seed as well as products of primary processing which contain cereals or products which do not contain cereals but are directly interchangeable in their use with cereals for example starch from potatoes or with products obtained from cereals.[2]

The three prices for cereals are fixed as follows:

	1993/94[3]	1994/95	1995/96 onwards
Target price (ECUs per tonne)	130	120	110
Threshold price (ECUs per tonne)	175	165	155
Intervention price (ECUs per tonne)	117	108	100

Intervention is available for common wheat, durum wheat, rye, barley, maize and sorghum provided that conditions of quality and quantity are met. Import levies based on the threshold price of each product less the cif price are charged on imports of cereals[4] and export refunds are granted on exports based on the difference between world market prices and community prices.[5]

The effect of these reforms on market prices received by farmers is complicated by a change in the standards required for intervention and by the green pound devaluations.

Under the old regime intervention operated for common wheat, which is essentially bread-making wheat, with supplements paid for differing qualities.[6] Feed quality wheat and barley were also available for intervention at a reduced number of ECUs compared to common wheat. Under the new regime intervention applies to common wheat and to barley at the same number of ECUs so that feed wheat is excluded from intervention.

This raises some concerns about the lack of a market of last resort for UK wheat. However, some concessions were made in setting new quality

---

1　As defined in Council Regulation 1765/92.
2　Article 1 and Annex A of Council Regulation 1766/92.
3　The Cereals Year starts on July 1. Therefore, the 1993/94 marketing year relates to the 1993 harvest, ie the crops sown in either autumn 1992 or spring 1993 and harvested in the summer/autumn of 1993 and usually marketed in the summer/autumn 1993 or spring 1994.
4　Articles 9 and 10 of Council Regulation 1766/92.
5　Articles 9 and 13 of Council Regulation 1766/92.
6　Commission Regulation 1570/77.

standards for common wheat, which will make it slightly easier for UK wheat to qualify for intervention. UK wheat had always had particular problems passing the notorious "machinability" test and the new rules allow wheat with a Zeleny index of at least 30 to forego the machinability test. Wheat scoring with a Zeleny index of 20 – 30 still has to pass a machinability test.

There was also some tightening of physical quality criteria. The maximum percentage of impaired grain allowable has been cut from 12% to 10%. The maximum quantity of impurities allowed has been cut from 12% to 7%.

These standards should allow most UK Group I (bread-making wheat) and some Group II (other hard wheat varieties) into intervention. The Commission did, however, also make the following statement regarding special intervention measures for feed wheat, which can be taken under Article 5 of the Council Regulation 1766/92:

> If the price of feed wheat were to fall to a level which risks disturbing the market for bread-making wheat or feed barley the Commission would take appropriate actions under Article 6 of Regulation 1766/92. An indication of the risk of such disturbance would be a discount on the market price for feed wheat by comparison with that for bread-making wheat or barley exceeding 5% at a time when intervention for wheat or barley was open and the market price for bread-making wheat or barley was at or below intervention price.

The success of UK wheat exports in recent years has been the competitive price in the autumn period. While continental wheat (mostly of bread-making quality) is kept in store waiting for higher intervention prices, UK wheat, although not of intervention standard, has attracted keen demand because of its general quality and price competitiveness. The new arrangements should mean that UK wheat remains in much the same position, which it would not have done had the single wheat standard been based on feed quality.

As an indication of the size of the support cuts the intervention buying-in price for barley is used:

	1992/93	1993/94	1994/95	1995/96
Intervention – ECUs/tonne	146	117	108	100
% change based on 1992/3	–	-20.0%	-26.0%	-31.5%

As already indicated in the introduction, the green pound devaluations gave UK farmers a considerable increase in price over the 1992/93 selling season. For 1993/94 the effect of the devaluations will be wiped out by the cut in ECUs so that at current conversion rates the basic support prices would be:

	1992/93	1993/94	1994/95	1995/96
Basic intervention (July) ECU/tonne	146	117	108	100
Green pound	0.795423	0.980715	0.980715	0.980715
Basic intervention £/tonne	116.13	114.74	105.92	98.07
Basic intervention allowing for reducing coefficient	116.13	113.31	104.59	96.84

Intervention support will fall by about £20/tonne by 1995/96 assuming current green pound rates. If the green pound revalues the fall would be greater. Without the devaluation of the green pound between 1992/93 and 1995/96, the fall would have been about £37/tonne. How actual market prices will change remains to be seen. The objective is that intervention will become the market of last resort again and that for the most part cereals will trade at prices between intervention and target.

These falls in price will, of course, be compensated. The calculation done by the Commission to arrive at the basic compensation was as follows:

	1993/94 ECU/t	1994/95 ECU/t	1995/96 ECU/t
Average 1992/93 price	155	155	155
Planned target price	130	120	110
Shortfall (giving basic amount of compensation)	25	35	45

See para 5.5 for further details of the compensation payment.

Monthly increments of 1.5 ECUs per tonne have been added to the basic intervention price from November to May under the old regime. At the time of writing it looks as if the Council will vote to reduce the increment to 1.35 ECUs per tonne for the 1993/94 marketing year.

3.2   The common market in oil seeds[1]

The common organisation for oil seeds[2] is based on a system of area subsidies to Community growers. This enables oil seeds to be traded within the Community at close to world price level but at the same time keeps Community producers in a position to grow oil seeds by ensuring that the return to producers is comparable to that which they receive from growing cereals. Since cereal prices in the community are kept artificially high by virtue of intervention and threshold price support there needs to be an oil seeds support system to producers which is provided via annual area payments.

The movement towards world prices results from a decision of a GATT panel in December 1989, known as the SOYA panel, upholding US criticism of the EC oil seeds regime. The EC accepted the panel's conclusions and agreed to modify its scheme.

Initially Council Regulation 3766/91 established a new system of support for oil seed producers to be applied with effect from the crops harvested in 1992.

In turn this has now been superseded by Council Regulation 1765/92 for oil seeds for harvest after July 1 1993.[3]

---

1   As defined in Council Regulation 1765/92.
2   See Council Regulations 136/66 and 1491/85.
3   Article 17 of Council Regulation 1765/92.

The effect of the reorganisation of the oil seeds market on prices actually received by farmers has been dramatic. Under the old regime (operating before the 1992 harvest) the subsidy was paid to oil seed crushers, who passed on the subsidy in the purchase price paid to farmers. Typically the price paid to farmers for oil seed rape in the early autumn of 1990 and 1991 was £260 and £220 per tonne respectively. In 1992 the price was £110 per tonne prior to the collapse of sterling. Compensation paid to growers in England for the 1992 crop was £398.63 per ha. Thus the total returns compare as follows:

	1991/92	1992/93
Yield – T/ha	3.08	3.08
Price – £/T	220	110
	£/ha	**£/ha**
Sales	678	339
Area payment	–	399
Total	678	738

Total returns depend on both yield and price received. At the yield and prices used in the calculation above, growers were fully compensated for the 1992 crop following the change in support. Prospects for 1993 are for both higher world market prices and higher payments because of green pound changes. For a full explanation of the payment for crops harvested in 1993 onwards please refer to para 5 dealing with area compensatory payments for oil seeds.

3.3   The common market in proteins[1]

The situation for protein crops is similar to that of oil seeds in that the old regime paid a subsidy to the processor who passed it on to the farmer. Farmers will sell at world market prices for the first time in 1993 and the effect is expected to be approximately a halving of the price received in 1992. For details of the compensation please refer to para 5 dealing with area compensatory payments for proteins.

The provisions of Council Regulation 1431/82 are now replaced by Council Regulation 1765/92 for protein crops to be harvested after July 1 1993.[2] This book only deals with those crops harvested after July 1 1993, but Council Regulation 1431/82 continues to apply to protein crops harvested in 1992 and sold before June 30 1993.[3]

There is provision which would allow the arrangements for making compensatory payments for oil seeds apply to protein crops from the 1994/95 marketing year onwards.[4]

---

1   As defined in Council Regulation 1765/92.
2   Article 17.2 of Council Regulation 1765/92.
3   Article 17.2 of Council Regulation 1765/92.
4   Article 15.2 of Council Regulation 1765/92.

An outline of the new system

4   Council Regulation 1765/92 establishes a new support system for arable farmers hinged around the concept of reducing community prices to world market prices and compensating the consequent loss of income with compensatory payments to producers. It imposes a harmonised system of compensation across all the main arable crops consisting of cereals, oil seeds and proteins.

The means of doing this is to pay compensation to producers growing qualifying arable crops on restricted areas of land ("eligible land"). The amount of the compensation for cereals and proteins is calculated by multiplying a rate per tonne by average cereal yields in regions determined by Member States. The amount of compensation for set-aside land is based on a notional use of the land for cereals production. The amount of compensation for oil seeds is based on an area payment multiplied by a fraction reflecting average regional yield and average community yield. Regional base areas are determined by reference to the average areas used to grow arable crops or set-aside. If the total area on which compensation payments are claimed exceeds the regional base area, payments to producers in that region are reduced in that year and an uncompensated set-aside requirement is imposed for the following year.

The new system applies from the marketing year 1993/94 onwards and the marketing year runs from July 1 to June 30.[1]

It is a voluntary system. Arable crops may still be grown on non-eligible land but no compensation will be paid.

With a view to facilitating administration and control there are two alternative schemes for claiming compensatory payments. The first is called the "general scheme" and the second is called the "simplified scheme". The second is open to small producers,[2] but anyone can be a small producer if he choses.[3]

Under the general scheme producers are obliged to set-aside a predetermined percentage of the arable land they wish to claim for as a condition of receiving compensation on the balance. Producers can choose how much of their eligible land they claim on. For example, if they wish they can claim just on their proteins and oil seed crops, but not on their cereals. Initially the rate of set-aside has been set at 15%. Producers are compensated for complying with this obligation.

Council Regulation 1765/92 gave Member States the option of allocating individual base areas for each producer's holding but the UK has not taken up this option.[4] Subsequent recourse to the individual base area system is however permitted.[5]

Under the simplified scheme there is no obligation to set-aside, but

---

1 Article 1 of Council Regulation 1765/92.
2 Eleventh Recital and Article 8 of Council Regulation 1765/92.
3 See "The simplified scheme" below.
4 Para 3 of Article 2 of Council Regulation 1765/92.
5 Para 4 of Article 2 of Council Regulation 1765/92.

producers still receive compensation. The simplified scheme is likely to be taken up by a relatively small proportion of UK farmers compared with the rest of Europe.

Area compensatory payments

5.1   Eligible land

Compensatory payments can only be made in respect of land which is down to arable crops or subject to the set-aside scheme under the new scheme and which is eligible. For land to be eligible it must not have been under permanent pasture, permanent crops, forest or non-agricultural uses on December 31 1991.[1]

The significance of land use at December 31 1991 should be recognised. The value of land that is eligible to receive area payments for the foreseeable future is likely to be affected. Certainly land not able to be registered as eligible will decrease in value unless it has some other specialist use (such as for beef or sheep production in the hands of producers with relevant quota). Registration of land will be made in the IACS return by May 15 1993 and all occupiers or landowners are encouraged to make sure eligible land is registered even if area payments are not being claimed. Although preferable to register in 1993, a later registration is not precluded.

Permanent pasture is defined as "non-rotational land used for grass production (sown or natural) on a permanent basis (five years or longer)".[2] In the MAFF Arable Area Payments booklet (AR2), permanent pasture is described as rough grazing (including moorland) and any area which had been in grass for five years or more at December 31 1991. This means land in temporary grass at December 31 1991 is counted as eligible land, so long as it was sown on or after January 1 1987 and was part of an arable rotation. Pasture reseeded since January 1 1987 does not qualify if the land has not been in an arable rotation.

Permanent crops are defined as "non-rotational crops other than permanent pasture that occupy the ground for five years or longer and yield repeated harvests".[3] Examples would be nursery crops, trees and bushes for fruit and berry production, vines, hops and glasshouse or polytunnel crops.

Exceptions to the above "five-year rule" are allowed for both permanent pasture and permanent crops where it can be shown that a field has been in a genuine arable rotation. Special forms must be submitted showing the cropping history for the years 1982 – 1992 of the fields in question, as well as all the other fields in the arable rotation. A declaration has to be signed which includes the granting of permission to use census returns and any other records to confirm the application.

An exception also applies to land on which payments were legitimately claimed under the transitional oilseeds regime. It was possible to claim under this scheme (applying to the 1992 harvest year) on land ploughed out of permanent pasture between December 31 1991 and March 15 1992.

---

1   Article 9 of Council Regulation 1765/92.
2   Article 3 and Annex to Commission Regulation 2780/92.
3   Article 3 and Annex to Commission Regulation 2780/92.

5.2   Arable crops

The support system for arable crops applies to the following:[1]

CN Code
Cereals

1001 10	Durum wheat
1001 90	Other wheat and meslin other than durum wheat
1002 00 00	Rye
1003 00	Barley
1004 00	Oats
1005	Maize
1007 00	Grain Sorghum
1008	Buckwheat, millet and canary seeds; other cereals
0709 90 60	Sweetcorn

Oil seeds

1201 00	Soya beans
1205 00	Rape seed[2]
1206 00	Sunflower seed

Protein crops[3]

0713 10	Peas
0713 50	Field beans
1209 29 50	Sweet lupins

5.2.1   Cereals

The minimum area that may be claimed for cereals in any application[4] is 0.3 ha and Member States can regulate the minimum plot area.[5] In the UK plots must be at least 0.1 ha or 0.01 ha in the case of seed production or research.[6] The sowing of the crop has to be done fully and in line with local recognised standards and maintained until at least the beginning of flowering in normal growth conditions.[7] This prevents a very thin sowing followed by minimal husbandry and no harvest merely to gain entitlement to compensatory payments. At present sowing must be completed by May 15 although May 31 may become the deadline for sweetcorn and sunflowers (England and Wales) and for forage maize (UK).[8] These general rules apply to oil seeds and protein crops also.

---

1 Annex 1 of Council Regulation 1765/92 as extended by Commission Regulation 2467/92 and amended by Commission Regulation 3738/92.
2 See Article 11 of Council Regulation 1765/92 and Article 3 of Commission Regulation 2294/92 and Article 1 of Commission Regulation 3529/92.
3 By Article 1.2(a) of Commission Regulation 2295/92 these are defined as arable crops producing protein seeds referred to in Annex 1 of Council Regulation 1765/92.
4 Under either the general or simplified schemes.
5 Article 4.3 of Commission Regulation 2780/92.
6 Para 15 of MAFF Arable Area Payments (AR2).
7 Article 4 of Commission Regulation 2780/92.
8 Annex 2, para 26 IACS 1.

5.2.2   Oil seeds

Oil seeds require some further explanation. Compensatory payments can only be made when the crop is grown in areas climatically and agronomically suitable to the cultivation of oil seed crops.[1] Scotland and Northern Ireland have been declared unsuitable for the purpose of growing sunflower seeds and soya beans, but the whole of the UK is deemed suitable for the approved[2] varieties of rape seed. A crop only counts as an oil seed crop if it is sown on or before May 15 prior to the marketing year[3] except in exceptional circumstances due to climatic conditions which need special clearance.[4]

The minimum size of sowing is 0.3 ha and Member States can determine the minimum size of each cultivated parcel.[5] This is the same as for cereals in the UK ie 0.1 ha. Not only do crops have to be grown with seed of approved variety,[6] but also the seed must comply with a strict quality policy.[7] There are specific rules for farm produced seed, high erucic acid rape for industrial use and seed grown for use as seed for sowing, research or testing purposes to determine whether the stock may be added to a Member State's national variety list. Growers are required to keep invoices and seed labels for inspection.

No area aid is payable on land where the rape seed sown does not meet these criteria.[8] Oil seed crops have to be maintained, which means properly husbanded according to local standard farming methods, until at least the beginning of flowering in normal growth conditions and until at least June 30 prior to the marketing year in which the crop will be sold. The only exception is where harvest takes place before June 30.[9] Oil seed crops are only eligible for compensatory payments at the prescribed rate for oil seeds if they are claimed under the general scheme.

5.2.3   Proteins

Protein crops are only eligible for compensatory payments at the prescribed rate for proteins[10] if:
- they are claimed for under the general scheme[11]
- grown in a region which is declared climatically and agronomically suitable.[12] The whole of the UK is suitable

---

1 Article 2.1(a) of Commission Regulation 2294/92.
2 See Article 11.1 of Council Regulation 1765/92 and Article 3 of Commission Regulation 2294/92.
3 Article 1.2(a) and Annex 1 of Commission Regulation 2294/92 .
4 Article 2.2 of Commission Regulation 2294/92.
5 See Article 2.1(e) of Commission Regulations 2294/92 and 3368/92.
6 See Article 3.1(a) and Annex II of Commission Regulation 2294/92 as amended by Commission Regulations 3529/92 and 819/93.
7 See Article 11.1 of Council Regulation 1765/92 and Article 3.1 and Annexes III, IV and V of Commission Regulation 615/92.
8 Article 9.5 of Commission Regulation 3887/92
9 Article 1a of Commission Regulation 2294/92 as amended by Commission Regulation 819/93.
10 Article 6 of Council Regulation 1765/92.
11 Article 2(b) of Commission Regulation 2295/92.
12 Article 2(a) of Commission Regulation 2295/92.

- covered by an application lodged with the competent authority by May 15 at the latest[1]
- they were sown by May 15 at the latest[2]
- the total area in the application is not less than 0.3 ha and each cultivated plot exceeds a minimum size to be laid down by Member States
- grown according to locally recognised standards.

5.2.4   Linseed

Linseed grown for seed is not currently an arable crop for the purpose of the area compensatory payment system under Council Regulation 1765/92. There is a separate support system for linseed grown for seed,[3] but there is a strong expectation that linseed will be brought within the area compensatory system for the 1994 crop and indications are that support would be reduced dramatically to 75 ECUs per ha for the 1994 crop. Whatever the Council finally determine in respect of payment for linseed in 1993 and thereafter there will be no set-aside requirement for linseed in 1993.[4] The current proposal is to treat linseed as a protein crop. There is also a support system for growers of fibre flax and hemp which is part of the fibres sector.[5]

5.2.5   Vining peas

Vining peas have had a somewhat uncertain history. Originally[6] they were not in the arable aid system. They were then introduced[7] but subsequently removed.[8] It follows that peas for the purpose of defining arable crop means only those peas sown with the intention of harvesting them in their dry state at full agricultural ripeness.[9]

To cope with this confusion on January 6 1993 a derogation was announced for producers to take into account their legitimate expectation that vining peas would be included. The derogation is granted to producers who acted on the decision to include vining peas and sowed or made commitments to sow vining peas before November 17 1992. Those producers are eligible for the area compensatory payments on both their vining peas and related set-aside land. However, proof of commitment is required at the time of application. A further derogation was announced by David Curry, Minister of State at the Ministry of Agriculture, Fisheries and Food (MAFF) on February 17 1993 stating that those producers who want to avail themselves of the first derogation but would be unable to do so because they had ploughed their set-aside land in the reasonable belief that vining peas were excluded would not be liable to penalties for having ploughed the set-aside land.

---

1 Article 2(c) of Commission Regulation 2295/92.
2 Article 2(d) of Commission Regulation 2295/92.
3 Council Regulation 569/76.
4 MAFF Press Release 96/93 of March 22 1993.
5 See Council Regulations 1308/70 and 619/71.
6 Annex 1 of Council Regulation 1765/92.
7 Commission Regulation 2467/92.
8 Commission Regulation 3738/92.
9 Article 2 Commission Regulation 3738/92.

5.2.6   Maize

Maize is classified as a cereal[1] but Member States can apply the yield for another food cereal if maize is grown principally for silage in a region.[2] The UK has not opted to apply another food cereal yield.

5.2.7   Mixed crops

Where cereals are mixed with oil seeds or proteins compensatory payments are made at the cereals rate.[3]

5.3   Regional base areas

For the purposes of defining regional base areas regions are either Member States or regions within Member States. Member States were given the freedom to decide. The original base area in a region is determined by taking the average number of hectares in the region down to arable crops or in a set-aside scheme during 1989, 1990 and 1991.[4] The UK has been split into five regions and the regional base areas are[5]

Regions	Base areas '000 ha
England	3742
Wales	61
N. Ireland	53
Scotland	
– LFA	160
– Non LFA	391

5.4   Regionalisation and average yields

The UK had to submit a regionalisation plan to the Commission by August 1 1992[6] in which the UK was broken down into regions so as to determine average yields for cereals, oil seeds and protein crops. The average was determined by looking at the five-year period 1986/87 to 1990/91. The cereals and where possible the oil seeds yields were calculated separately excluding the years with the highest and lowest yields in that period.[7]

In drawing up the regionalisation plan to establish separate production regions the criteria used by Member States had to be "appropriate, objective and provide the necessary flexibility for the recognition of distinct homogeneous zones, which are of a minimum size and allow for specific characteristics that influence yields such as soil fertility, including

---

1   Annex 1 of Council Regulation 1765/92.
2   Article 9 of Commission Regulation 2780/92.
3   Article 8 of Commission Regulation 2780/92.
4   Para 2 Article 2 of Council Regulation 1765/92.
5   Article 1 and Annex to Commission Regulation 845/93.
6   Para 3 of Article 3 of Council Regulation 1765/92.
7   Para 2 of Article 3 of Council Regulation 1765/92.

when appropriate due differentiation between irrigated and non-irrigated areas".[1]

The regional average yield figures produced for the UK are

	Cereals/proteins tonnes per ha	Oil seeds tonnes per ha
England	5.93	3.08
Wales	4.65	3.14
N Ireland	4.71	2.92
Scotland		
– LFA	4.81	2.84
– Non-LFA	5.65	3.49

Formal Commission approval has not yet been received for the UK's regionalisation plan but MAFF believe that this is a formality.

The financial implications of drawing the regional boundaries in this way can be marked and it could be argued somewhat arbitrary in some cases. As an example, take two identical 200-ha farms at either end of the Severn Bridge. No measurable yield differences would be expected between these farms in practice, but for the purpose of this scheme the English farm has a much higher cereal and protein average yield although the Welsh farm does slightly better with oilseeds. On a typical all combinable crop rotation the compensation figures for the 1993 crop would be:

	ha	per ha	England £	per ha	Wales £
Cereals	102 @	£145.39	14,830 @	£114.01	11,629
Proteins	34 @	£378.02	12,853 @	£296.42	10,078
Oilseeds	34 @	£459.49	15,623 @	£468.44	15,927
Set-aside	30 @	£261.70	7,851 @	£205.21	6,156
	200		51,157		43,790

The benefit of being on the english side of the bridge in this example is £7,367 in 1993, or £36.83/ha (£14.90/acre). The cereal compensation payments increase for the following two years so that the gap widens in 1994 to £8,646 and in 1995 to £9,926 or £20/acre. The implications of this for land values and rent reviews is obvious.

5.5   The formula for payment

5.5.1   Cereals

The cereals compensatory payment is calculated by multiplying the basic amount per tonne by the average regional cereals yield.[2]

The basic amount per tonne is:

---

1   Para 3 of Article 3 of Council Regulation 1765/92.
2   Para 1 of Article 4 of Council Regulation 1765/92.

Marketing year 1993/94	25 ECUs
Marketing year 1994/95	35 ECUs
Marketing year 1995/96 onwards	45 ECUs

Thus, the payment to producers in England in the marketing year 1993/94 is

| Basic amount | x | the regional average yield |
| (25 ECUs per tonne) | | (5.93 tonnes per ha) |

x green pound conversion rate = £145.39 per ha
(1 ECU = £0.980715)

For the UK the comparable figures are

| | Cereal aid payments in £s per ha | | |
	1993/94	1994/95	1995/96 onwards
England	145.39	203.55	261.70
Wales	114.01	159.61	205.21
N Ireland	115.48	161.67	207.86
Scotland			
– LFA	117.93	165.10	212.28
– Non LFA	138.53	193.94	249.35

Note that, as previously stated, all these figures are based on a green pound conversion rate of £0.980715 to 1 ECU and this figure will fluctuate. The actual rate of conversion to be used is expected to be that applying on July 1 1993.[1] Further note that the Community has the power to alter the amounts of all the compensatory payments "in the light of developments in production, productivity and the markets".[2]

5.5.2   Proteins

The basic amount is fixed at 65 ECUs per tonne for 1993/94 onwards. The regional yield figure utilised is the same as the cereals figure[3] giving a proteins compensatory payment of

| Basic amount | x | regional average yield |
| (65 ECUs per tonne) | | (5.93 tonnes per ha) |

x green pound conversion rate = £378 per ha
(1 ECU = £0.980715)

For the UK the comparable figures are

	1993/94 onwards £s per ha
England	378.02
Wales	296.42
N Ireland	300.25
Scotland	
– LFA	306.62
– Non-LFA	360.17

1 Article 10 of Commission Regulation 2780/92.
2 Article 15 of Council Regulation 1765/92.
3 Article 6 of Council Regulation 1765/92.

Note that, as previously stated, all the figures are based on a green pound conversion rate of £0.980715 and this figure will fluctuate. The actual rate of conversion to be used is expected to be that applying on July 1 1993.[1] Further note that the Community has the power to alter the amounts of all the compensatory payments "in the light of developments in production, productivity and the markets".[2]

5.5.3   Oil seeds

The calculation for the compensatory payment for oil seeds is different to cereals and proteins.[3] It is more flexible and built into the formula is the ability to adjust the payment rates if world prices (quaintly known as the "observed reference price") differ significantly from the anticipated world price (the projected reference price).

The projected reference price for oil seeds is set at 163 ECUs per tonne.[4] The EC Commission believes that the price relationship between oil seeds and cereals should be 2.1:1. The overall price to producers (including EC support) is therefore calculated by multiplying the EC cereals price by 2.1. The overall price less world price per tonne then leaves the support level per tonne.

Thus for 1993 the calculation which led to determination of the community reference amount of 359 ECUs per hectare was:

Expected world price for cereals	100 ECUs per tonne
Cereals compensatory payment (mistakenly estimated at)	50 ECUs per tonne
Equivalent EC cereal price	150 ECUs per tonne

Applying the equilibrium price relationship of 2.1:1 gives an oil seeds price figure of 315 ECUs per tonne.

From this has to be deducted the estimated world price of 163 ECUs per tonne requiring an EC oil seeds compensatory payment of 152 ECUs per tonne.

The EC's average yield for oil seeds is 2.36 tonnes per ha meaning that the rate of compensation per hectare needs to be 359 ECUs per ha.

The community reference amount for oil seeds is set at 359 ECUs per ha for the 1993/94 marketing year onwards.[5] Member States then have to determine in each region a projected regional reference amount by a fraction consisting of either:

$$\frac{\text{Cereals yield for the specific region}}{\text{the average cereals yield for the community}}$$
(4.6 tonnes per ha)

OR

$$\frac{\text{Oil seeds yield for the specific region}}{\text{the average oil seeds yield for the community}}$$
(2.36 tonnes per ha)[6]

---

1   Article 5 of Commission Regulation 2295/92 as amended by Commission Regulation 2891/92.
2   Article 15 of Council Regulation 1765/92.
3   Article 5 of Council Regulation 1765/92.
4   Article 5.1(a) of Council Regulation 1765/92.
5   Article 5.1 of Council Regulation 1765/92.
6   Article 5.1(c) of Council Regulation 1765/92.

The UK has opted for the second formula.

The regional average oil seed yield figures in the UK are set at:

Oil seeds tonnes per ha

England	3.08
Wales	3.14
N Ireland	2.92
Scotland	
– LFA	2.84
– Non-LFA	3.49

The compensatory payment is then calculated in the following way:

Community reference amount   x   the projected regional amount
(£359 ECUs per ha)

$$\frac{\text{(3.08 tonnes per ha (England))}}{\text{(2.36 tonnes per ha)}} \quad \text{x} \quad \text{the green pound conversion}$$
rate (1 ECU = £0.980715)

= £459.49 per ha

For the UK the comparable figures are:

Oil seeds compensatory payment	£s per ha
England	459.49
Wales	468.44
N Ireland	435.62
Scotland	
– LFA	423.69
– Non-LFA	520.66

Note that, as previously stated, all the figures are based on a green pound conversion rate of £0.980715 and this figure will fluctuate. The actual rate of conversion to be used is expected to be that applying on July 1 1993.[1] Further note that the Community has the power to alter the amounts of all the compensatory payments "in the light of developments in production, productivity and the markets".[2]

5.5.4   Set-aside

Initially the compensatable area of set-aside is set at 15% of each producer's eligible land down to arable crops for which a claim is made and including the set-aside area.[3] Alternatively, the set-aside area required is 17.65% of the actual area of arable crops claimed.

The compensation is fixed at the 1995/96 cereals level (45 ECUs per tonne) as if cereals were being grown.[4] Accordingly, the regional average cereals yields are applied to the basic amount.

Basic amount for cereals for 1995/96   x   the regional average cereals yield
(45 ECUs per tonne)   (5.93 tonnes per ha – England)

---

1   Article 8 of Commission Regulation 2294/92.
2   Article 15 of Council Regulation 1765/92.
3   Article 7.1 of Council Regulation 1765/92.
4   Article 7.5 of Council Regulation 1765/92.

x green pound conversion rate　　= £261.70 per ha
(1 ECU = £0.980715)

The figures for the UK are:

	1993/94 onwards £s per ha
England	261.70
Wales	205.21
N Ireland	207.86
Scotland	
– LFA	212.28
– Non-LFA	249.35

Note that, as previously stated, all the figures are based on a green pound conversion rate of £0.980715 and this figure will fluctuate. The actual rate of conversion to be used is expected to be that applying on July 1 1993. Further note that the Community has the power to alter the amounts of all the compensatory payments "in the light of developments in production, productivity and the markets".[1]

Compensation for land set-aside is only paid for the number of hectares needed to satisfy the set-aside requirement (15% of the area down to arable crops for which a claim is made but including the set-aside area).[2]

Land already set-aside in compliance with an earlier EC set-aside scheme[3] cannot be counted to meet the set-aside requirement.[4]

In addition to having to be eligible land,[5] land for set-aside has to meet further tests.[6]

5.5.5　Summary

Overall the complete picture for compensatory payments for arable crops in ECUs is set out below:

Arable area aid payments in ECUs per ha					
	Cereals			Set-aside	Proteins	Oil seeds
Harvest year	1993	1994	1995	1993–	1993–	1993–
England	148.25	207.55	266.85	266.85	385.45	468.53
Wales	116.25	162.75	209.25	209.25	302.25	477.65
N Ireland	117.75	164.85	211.95	211.95	306.15	444.19
Scotland						
– LFA	120.25	168.35	216.45	216.45	312.65	432.02
– Non-LFA	141.25	197.75	254.25	254.25	367.25	530.89

Subject to the same warnings as previously given about green pound conversion rates the equivalent sterling figures per hectare are:

1　Article 15 of Council Regulation 1765/92.
2　Article 7.5 of Council Regulation 1765/92.
3　Article 2 of Council Regulation 2328/91.
4　Article 7.2 of Council Regulation 1765/92.
5　See Article 9 of Council Regulation 1765/92 above.
6　See "What land can be used for set aside" and Article 9 of Council Regulation 1765/92.

Harvest year	Cereals			Set-aside	Proteins	Oil seeds
	1993	1994	1995	1993–	1993–	1993–
England	145.39	203.55	261.70	261.70	378.02	459.49
Wales	114.01	159.61	205.21	205.21	296.42	468.44
N Ireland	115.48	161.67	207.86	207.86	300.25	435.62
Scotland						
– LFA	117.93	165.10	212.28	212.28	306.62	423.69
– Non-LFA	138.53	193.94	249.35	249.35	360.17	520.66

Arable area aid payments in £s per ha (1 ECU = £0.980715)

The equivalent sterling figures per acre are:

Harvest year	Cereals			Set-aside	Proteins	Oil seeds
	1993	1994	1995	1993–	1993–	1993–
England	58.84	82.37	105.91	105.91	152.98	185.45
Wales	46.14	64.59	83.05	83.05	119.96	189.58
N Ireland	46.73	65.43	84.12	84.12	121.51	176.29
Scotland						
– LFA	47.73	66.82	85.91	85.91	124.09	171.46
– Non-LFA	56.06	78.48	100.91	100.91	145.76	210.71

Arable area aid payments in £s per acre (1 ECU = £0.980715)

At the time of writing a revaluation of the green pound seems more likely than further devaluations. Assuming a 15% revaluation, the compensation payments would be:

Harvest year	Cereals			Set-aside	Proteins	Oil seeds
	1993	1994	1995	1993–	1993–	1993–
England	50.01	70.01	90.02	90.02	130.03	158.06
Wales	39.22	54.90	70.59	70.59	101.97	161.14
N Ireland	39.73	55.62	71.50	71.50	103.28	149.85
Scotland						
– LFA	40.57	56.80	73.02	73.02	105.48	145.74
– Non-LFA	47.65	66.71	85.77	85.77	123.90	179.10

Arable area aid payments in £s per acre
Assuming a 15% revaluation to 1 ECU = £0.8336078

5.6   The simplified scheme

So far we have only considered the general scheme which is open to all producers and involves mandatory 15% set-aside.[1] There is also a simplified scheme open to small producers.[2] Under the simplified scheme there is no requirement to set-aside land and area compensatory payments are paid at the cereals rate for all areas sown to arable crops regardless of whether they are proteins or oil seeds.[3]

However, the definition of small producers is so vague that it would be more appropriate to describe the simplified scheme as being open to small claimants. A large producer who only makes a small claim for compensatory payments is able to utilise the simplified scheme.

A small producer is one who makes a claim for compensatory

1 Article 2.5 of Council Regulation 1765/92.
2 Article 2.5 of Council Regulation 1765/92.
3 Article 8.3 of Council Regulation 1765/92.

payments for an area no bigger than that which would be needed to produce 92 tonnes of cereals.[1] In England the regional average yield for cereals is 5.93 tonnes per ha which means that small producers can claim for a maximum of 15.51 ha or 38.3 acres of arable crops grown on eligible land.

The figures for the UK are:

Small producers	ha	acres
England	15.51	38.33
Wales	19.78	48.88
N Ireland	19.53	48.26
Scotland		
– LFA	19.12	47.26
– Non-LFA	16.28	40.23

Payment is made at the rate for cereals and accordingly the maximum payments are

1993   92 tonnes x 25 ECUs x green pound conversion rate
       (1 ECU = £0.980715)
       = £2,255.64

1994   92 tonnes x 35 ECUs x green pound conversion rate
       (1 ECU = £0.980715)
       = £3,157.90

1995   92 tonnes x 45 ECUs x green pound conversion rate
       (1 ECU = £0.980715)
       = £4,060.16

Where a producer is applying under the simplified scheme and has land in more than one yield region, some careful juggling of figures may be necessary. The principle is that the total claim must be for areas of eligible land that would produce less than or up to 92 tonnes of grain at the relevant regional cereal yield. Thus if a producer has 10 ha in England, this would produce 10 x 5.93 tonnes per ha = 59.3 tonnes. This leaves 32.7 tonnes (92 – 59.3 tonnes) to be claimed in, say, Wales which at 4.65 tonnes per ha would require 7.03 ha.

5.7   Payments

Application can only be made for one compensatory payment for any piece of land in any marketing year and no other application for any per hectare aid can have been made.[2]

The compensatory payments for cereals, proteins and set-aside are to be paid between October 16 and December 31.[3]

Payment of the oil seeds compensatory payment is in two instalments for the time being. The first instalment is paid after planting and in the

---

1   Article 8.2 of Council Regulation 1765/92.
2   Article 2 of Commission Regulation 2780/92.
3   Article 10.1 of Council Regulation 1765/92.

UK is the maximum permitted amount which is 50% of the projected regional reference amount.[1] The advance payment has to be made at the earliest date possible and by September 30 in the marketing year by the latest.[2] Since that amount is not yet determinable because regionalisation plans for Member States are still provisional transitional measures have had to be adopted for winter rape.[3] To qualify, the producer must submit a sowing claim by a specified date together with supporting documentation.[4] In 1993 this will be part of the producer's IACS form to be submitted by May 15.

The balance is the difference between the amount of the advance and the final regional reference amount. It is payable after harvest of the crop.[5] There is the possibility of an orderly market bonus being paid if the producer delays selling the crop.[6] This bonus has not been paid in previous years, but discussions are due to take place this summer between Member States and the Commission to try to implement the system. Implementation is widely regarded as desirable in the interests of balancing the relevant bargaining positions of producers and merchants.

In calculating final compensatory payments due the price may be altered if the observed reference price differs from the projected reference price by more than 8%.[7] The final payment has to be made within 60 days of the final regional reference amounts being determined.[8]

So if the observed reference price in 1993 proves to be 180 ECUs per tonne instead of 163 ECUs per tonne the EC compensatory payment will be reduced to 148 ECUs per tonne after allowing for the 8% tolerance. This means that the community reference amount would become 349 ECUs per ha instead of 359 ECUs per ha and for the harvest in England this would mean that total payments became £446.69 per ha instead of £459.49 per ha.

For payments in respect of oil seeds made in the course of a marketing year the green pound conversion rate is that in force on the first day of the marketing year (July 1).[9] However, advances on payments made before July 1 are paid either at the rate in force on the last day for submission of application or at the rate in force at the date of submission.[10] If claiming for oil seeds under the simplified scheme (ie at cereals rate) the green pound conversion rate is that in force for cereals on the first day of the marketing year.

---

1 Article 11.2 of Council Regulation 1765/92.
2 Article 7a.3 of Commission Regulation 2294/92 as amended by Commission Regulation 819/93.
3 Commission Regulation 3368/92. French winter rape producers received an early advance on their autumn 1992 sown crops. This may be adopted in other Member States for the autumn 1993 sowings.
4 Article 11.3 of Council Regulation 1765/92.
5 Article 11.4 of Council Regulation 1765/92.
6 Article 11.5 of Council Regulation 1765/92.
7 Article 5.1(d) of Council Regulation 1765/92.
8 Article 7a.4 of Commission Regulation 2294/92 as amended by Commission Regulation 819/93.
9 Article 8.1 of Commission Regulation 2294/92.
10 Article 8.2 of Commission Regulation 2294/92.

The agricultural conversion rate for proteins is that prevailing on the first day of the marketing year[1] and if the claim is made under the simplified scheme the rate is that for cereals prevailing on the first day of the marketing year.[2]

The agricultural conversion rate for compensatory payments for cereals is the rate on July 1 of the marketing year.[3]

If a producer has eligible land in more than one region the amount to be paid is determined by the location of each area included in his application.[4]

5.8   Which scheme or none?

Whether a producer should choose between the general or the simplified scheme (or none) is a very individual decision, depending on a number of key variables such as crops grown, area involved and yield and price levels.

Neither oil seed nor protein area payments can be claimed under the simplified scheme so that, in general, if either of these crops is grown there is no choice but to claim under the general scheme. For both crops about 50% of the total return comes from the area payment, whereas for cereals, it is about 15% in 1993 rising to 30% in 1995.

For cereal-only claimants, there may be a decision to be made between the two schemes. The example below compares the returns at gross margin level for 1993 in a 40 ha cereal situation in England with yields at 7 tonne/ha, price at £110/tonne and variable costs at £220/ha.

	£
1. No scheme	
Gross margin 40 ha @ £550	22,000
2. Simplified scheme	
Gross margin 40 ha @ £550	22,000
Maximum area payment 15.51 ha @ £145.39	2,255
	24,255
3. General scheme	
Gross margin 34 ha @ £550	18,700
Set-aside 6 ha @ £261.70	1,570
Cereals area payment 34 ha @ £145.39	4,943
	25,213

In this example there is an advantage of £958 in opting for the general scheme rather than the simplified scheme and, in addition, some minor savings in fixed costs could be made from the area in set-aside.

Sensitivity analysis on this example shows that at these performance levels the break-even point comes at about 28 ha. At this or a lower area it would be better to opt for the simplified scheme. In most situations

---

1   Article 5 of Commission Regulation 2295/92 as amended by Commission Regulation 2891/92.
2   Article 5.2(c) of Commission Regulation 2295/92 as amended by Commission Regulation 2891/92.
3   Article 10 of Commission Regulation 2780/92.
4   Article 5 of Commission Regulation 2780/92.

in 1993, if the area grown is above 28 ha (70 acres), it is best to opt for the general scheme. By 1995 harvest the break-even point is likely to be closer to 20 ha (50 acres) because of the lower cereal prices being more fully compensated under the general scheme.

For no scheme to be better than the general scheme, yield would have to increase to 10.5 tonnes/ha and price to £125/tonne before a producer would be better off ignoring the general scheme. However, it is clear that the simplified scheme will always be better than no scheme as the area payment is always additional to the gross margin.

Note: The conversion rate used in the above example is 1 ECU = £0.980715. A change in rates will change both gross margin and compensation and will alter relative positions, but not significantly.

5.9 Exceeding the regional base area

It will be recalled from earlier in this chapter that land eligible to receive compensatory payments for growing arable crops or complying with set-aside requirements is limited to land not under permanent pasture, permanent crops, forest or non-agricultural uses on December 31 1991.[1] In addition it will be recalled that the concept of regional base areas for regions is the average number of hectares in a region either used for arable crops or set-aside in 1989, 1990 and 1991.[2] If in a marketing year the total area in a region for which aid is claimed (arable crops and set-aside) exceeds that region's base area then two things happen[3]:

(i) in that marketing year each producer's compensatory payments are reduced proportionately[4]
(ii) in the following marketing year producers in the general scheme will be required to put extra land aside (special set-aside) on top of the current 15% compensated set-aside requirement and they will receive no compensation for that special set-aside land. The amount of the special set-aside is the percentage amount by which the regional base area was exceeded in the previous year.

The proportionate reduction in compensatory payments applies to small producers as well as producers under the general scheme but the imposition of uncompensated set-aside is restricted to producers in the general scheme.[5]

The likelihood of exceeding the regional base area in 1993/94 seems low because the base is an average of three previous years, since when cropping areas have fallen. However, mixed farms in particular have the ability to tighten up their stocking rate on forage and grow more crops in order to make up for set-aside.

---

1 Article 9 of Council Regulation 1765/92.
2 Para 2 Article 2 of Council Regulation 1765/92.
3 Article 2.6 of Council Regulation 1765/92.
4 See Article 5 of Commission Regulation 2294/92 in respect of oil seeds.
5 Article 2.6 of Council Regulation 1765/92.

If this happens on a sufficient number of farms so that regional base area is exceeded, all farmers in that region will be penalised, whether or not they individually increase their cropping. As an example we take the 200 hectare English farm by the Severn Bridge in the previous chapter and assume a 2% excess on the regional base area.

(a) Effect in 1993/94

	£
Full compensation	
200ha @ average £255.78/ha	51,157
less 2% = 4 ha	
Adjusted compensation (200–4)	
196ha @ average £255.78/ha	50,133
Difference	1,024

(b) Effect in 1994/5

Budget with 15% set-aside

	Ha	Gross margin £/ha	£		Compensation £/ha	£	Total £
Cereals	102 @	525	53,550	@	203.55	20,762	74,312
Proteins	34 @	270	9,180	@	378.02	12,853	22,033
Oil seeds	34 @	270	9,180	@	459.49	15,623	24,803
Set-aside	30 @		–	@	261.70	7,851	7,851
	200		71,910			57,089	128,999

Budget with 15% set-aside plus 2% special set-aside

	Ha	Gross margin £/ha	£		Compensation £/ha	£	Total £
Cereals	100 @	525	52,500	@	203.55	20,355	72,855
Proteins	33 @	270	8,910	@	378.02	12,475	21,385
Oil seeds	33 @	270	8,910	@	459.49	15,163	24,073
Set-aside	30 @		–	@	261.70	7,851	7,851
Sp set-aside	4		–		–	–	–
	200		70,320			55,844	126,164
Difference			1,590			1,245	2,835

The example shows that, although there is no change in this farm's total cropping area, the effect of others increasing to trigger a 2% excess would be £1,024 less in compensation payments in 1993/94 and, in the following year, £2,835 less in gross margin and compensation.

5.10 Formalities

An application must be lodged by May 15 1993 and the crops sown by this date in order to qualify for area compensatory payments.[1] The details of what is required under the integrated administration and control system (IACS) for area aid applications are dealt with in detail in the section in this book under IACS.

The May 15 1993 sowing may be extended in some regions if the seasons justify it (this may apply to Scotland in some years).

---

1 Article 10.2 of Council Regulation 1765/92.

At least for the first year the area payment application has to include a map of the holding[1] printed on 1:10,000 or 1:2500 Ordnance Survey National Grid Map post-dating 1952, or a professionally produced estate map of the same standard and scale. Good photocopies of such maps are acceptable. Unless there are significant changes to the holding these maps will not have to be provided in subsequent years. The maps must show:

- the Ordnance Survey map number(s);
- the Ordnance Survey field sizes in hectares (not acres) for all eligible fields;
- four figure National Grid parcel numbers for all eligible fields. Older Ordnance Survey parcel numbers appearing on County series maps are unacceptable;
- all existing traditional buildings, stone walls, hedges, rows of trees including hedgerow trees, watercourses, ditches, ponds, pools, lochs and lakes which the producer is entitled to maintain and which are situated on or immediately adjacent to eligible fields. This is not necessary in Scotland.

Field measurements:
If whole fields are set-aside the OS field size may be used to calculate the set-aside area. Deductions need not be made for walls, hedges, or field margins but areas within the field that would not normally be cropped must be deducted. This includes rights of way, land around pylons, stands of trees, ponds or other features. Part fields and strips must be accurately measured.

The minimum size field on which aid can be claimed is 0.1 ha (unless used for seed production or research).

---

1 Article 10.3 of Council Regulation 1765/92.

Set-aside

6.1 Introduction

Council Regulation 1765/92 provided that set-aside land had to be rotated unless a non-rotational set-aside scheme was adopted. The price for entering into a non-rotational set-aside scheme is that a higher set-aside percentage rate is required. This rate has to be decided by the Council before 31 July 1993.[1]

Council Regulation 1765/92 provided that land set-aside under the general scheme could "be used for the provision of materials for the manufacture within the community of products not primarily intended for human or animal consumption, provided that effective control systems are applied".[2]

Detailed implementation of both these Council provisions is found in Commission Regulations 2293/92 and 334/93, which revoked 2296/92 as amended by 2941/92.

The rules relating to detailed implementation at Member State level have proved to be contentious and difficult to formulate. It is anticipated that further regulatory intervention will follow. The details of the EC non-rotational set-aside have not yet been determined.

6.2 Conditions relating to set-aside land

Commission Regulation 2293/92 lays down what land can be set-aside and deals with declarations and monitoring while Commission Regulation 334/93 lays down the rules for use of set-aside land for non-food production.

6.3 What land can be used for set-aside

In addition to having to meet the eligible status[3] land to be set-aside has to clear two other hurdles[4]:

(i) the land must have been farmed by the applicant for the two previous years. The exceptions to this rule are if:
  - during this period the producer inherits or succeeds to the land or takes the land in hand; or
  - the land forms part of a unit of at least 60 ha of agricultural land that has been purchased or rented or taken on a share farming agreement or under a licence approved by the Minister during this period. The land must have been acquired in a single transaction unless it previously formed part of the same unit of agricultural land; or

---

1 Article 7.1 of Council Regulation 1765/92.
2 Article 7.4 of Council Regulation 1765/92.
3 See Article 9 of Council Regulation 1765/92.
4 Article 3.4 of Commission Regulation 2293/92.

- during this period the land has been taken on (in the capacity of owner or on a tenancy from year to year or on a fixed term tenancy not approved by the Minister or as a share farmer or under a licence approved by the Minister) and the producer owns or rents no more than 15 ha of other agricultural land; or
- the land was let during any part of this period on a lease of less than two years, provided the producer normally farms the land; or
- more than 10% of the arable land which is farmed by the producer each year is normally share farmed or held on one or more agreements which constitute less than a tenancy from year to year. The land the producer intends to set-aside must be held or share farmed on the basis of such an arrangement, be geographically related to his other land and be able to be reasonably managed as a single unit with his other land; or, exceptionally
- the producer has insufficient land within the same yield region to meet his set-aside obligation in any other way.[1]

This provision was to prevent farmers purchasing or renting parcels of land (probably of poor quality) on which to dump their set-aside requirement.[2]

(ii) The land must have been cultivated in the previous year with a view to a harvest.[3] The one exception to this is land that was in either a five-year set-aside scheme or the one-year set-aside scheme for the 1992 harvest.[4] According to MAFF[5] only a combinable (including herbage seed) or root crop, which has been harvested by being cut or ploughed up and removed from the land is eligible. Crops left in or on the ground for grazing, while being identical crops are excluded. Furthermore land which was in temporary grass or lucerne in 1991/92 (even if the grass was used for hay or silage) or land which was not used to grow a harvestable crop for any other reason in 1991/92 is not eligible.[6] However, land in maize or other cereal crops cut for silage would be eligible and land which had a grass cover established by undersowing crops which were subsequently mechanically harvested in 1992 would apparently be eligible.

6.4   Fallow set-aside

Set-aside land has to be cared for to maintain good cropping conditions.[7]

---

1   Appendix 6 of MAFF explanatory booklet on arable regime and Annex 9 of MAFF explanatory booklet on IACS.
2   Third Recital of Commission Regulation 2293/92.
3   Article 2 of Commission Regulation 2293/92.
4   Council Regulations 1703/91 and 2328/92.
5   MAFF explanatory booklet p 17.
6   MAFF explanatory booklet p 17.
7   Article 3.2 of Commission Regulation 2293/92.

Member States are under an obligation to ensure protection of the environment,[1] and have to determine penalties for producers which are "appropriate and proportional" to the seriousness of the environmental consequences of not observing environmental protection measures.[2]

To comply with the set-aside requirement the land must be set-aside for a minimum period of seven months commencing at the earliest on December 15 and ending on August 15 at the latest.[3] The UK has adopted a set-aside period from December 15 to July 15 unless a producer has unharvested crops in the ground on December 15 in which case the period is January 15 to the August 15.

No parcel of land can be used for set-aside more than once in six years.[4] This rule applies whether or not the producer was farming the land when it was set-aside. Thus it will be important for future producers taking over any land to establish the set-aside history of land being bought or rented. The need for clear records is paramount.

Equally landlords letting eligible land on a short-term basis may need to consider what stipulations they should place on the land with regard to set-aside. If a short-term tenant used such land wholly for set-aside, this would prevent a future occupier from using the land for set-aside for six years. However, it is likely that this six-year rule will have to be changed. If set-aside is increased to 17% or any region has a special set-aside of 2% on top of the present basic 15%, then the six-year rule cannot stand because one year in six implies a maximum of 16.66% set-aside.

6.5   Fallow set-aside management rules

Interpretation of the Commission Regulation 2293/92 has been different in different parts of the UK and in different parts of the EC. This is only to be expected given the wide range of climatic and environmental conditions. However, the management rules for land put into set-aside have not always been spelt out clearly and changes can be expected.

The MAFF explanatory booklet (AR2) does have a section on management rules for set-aside land (Appendix I). A summary of the main rules is given below:

- a green cover crop over winter is required to reduce the risk of nitrate leaching. If crops were still in the ground at October 15 this requirement is waived. In Scotland no general winter cover requirement has been required.
- natural regeneration after a cereal crop is allowed so long as sufficient green cover establishes. Originally regeneration after burnt stubble was outlawed but later allowed where sufficient greening up occurred. No other clear guidance on what other cover crops were allowed

---

1   Article 3.3 of Commission Regulation 2293/92 and see Appendix 3 of MAFF explanatory booklet.
2   Article 3.3 of Commission Regulation 2293/92.
3   Article 3.4 of Commission Regulation 2293/92.
4   Article 3.5 of Commission Regulation 2293/92.

except that grass must be a mixture of at least two varieties with no more than 5% legumes and that game cover mixes must be in unharvestable mixtures.

- where crops were still in the ground at October 15, there is a choice of either establishing a spring cover crop or creating a bare summer fallow by June 1 at the latest.
- a bare summer fallow can be created in all circumstances after May 1 to control weeds. Thus most regenerated stubble will be ploughed in after May 1 to control both weeds and diseases.
- if cover is not ploughed in it must be cut at least once by July 1 and the cuttings left on the ground.
- no fertilisers can be applied (other than lime) but manure/slurry from the holding can be applied if there is a green cover.
- general use of pesticides is banned, although spot treatments to control weeds is permitted and derogation in other circumstances may be obtained.
- environmental features adjacent to set-aside land must be maintained.

All these rules apply to the seven-month period and in this time there must be no agricultural production or lucrative use. The Scottish office did mention that the grazing of the farmer's own horse(s) would be allowed and permission has been sought to hold the village fete on set-aside land (with no payment being allowed). Permission may be granted for draining land during its set-aside period.

Both immediately before and after the seven-month set-aside period use of the land is permitted (apart from heavy grazing prior to December 15 which might damage a green cover). This has resulted in mixed farms planning to use grass cover immediately after July 15 1993 for hay/silage or grazing which gives rise to the question whether this is against the "no agricultural production" rule. At the time of going to press the situation is unclear, although France has insisted that all cover crops must be destroyed at the end of the set-aside period. This may well be applied to the UK in 1994 if not in 1993.

6.6   Non-food or industrial use of set-aside land

Commission Regulation 334/93 sets up a complex system allowing set-aside land to be used to grow certain crops so long as the end use is primarily industrial and those crops are processed into acceptable non-food products. The producer receives the normal set-aside area compensatory payment, but can receive no other aid.[1]

The complex rules governing the relationship between the producer, collector and first processor and the copious requirements about formalities and the lodging of the documents with authorities are undoubtedly a disincentive to producers to go down this route, but despite the maze of red tape UK producers have opted to grow certain crops on set-aside land, notably bio-fuel crops and hemp. The growing

---

1   Article 5 of Commission Regulation 334/93.

of hemp[1] (cannabis sativa) requires a specific Home Office licence. Member States may refuse to permit certain crops to be grown either because they raise difficulties in terms of criminal law or in the areas of agricultural practice, control, public health or the environment.[2]

6.7   Definitions

Claimant, first processor and collector are defined.[3] The claimant is the producer who will receive the compensatory payments. The first processor is the user of the raw material who carries out the first processing with a view to obtaining one or more of the permitted products.[4] The collector is a party to the signed contract with the claimant buying the raw material on his own account for one of the permitted products.

6.8   Raw materials and end uses

The raw materials[5] which may be grown on set-aside land are:

CN Code

ex 0602 99 41	Short rotation forest trees having a maximum cultivation period of 10 years inclusive
0602 99 51	Outdoor perennial plants (eg Miscanthus sinesis)
0602 99 59	Other outdoor plants (eg Kenaf Hibiscus cannabinus L)
0701 90 10	Potatoes
ex 0713 10 90	Peas (Pisum sativum L) other than those for sowing
0713 50 90	Broad beans other than for sowing
0909 40 11	Seeds of caraway, neither crushed nor ground for the industrial manufacture of essential oils or resinoids
1001 90 99	Spelt, common wheat and meslin other than for sowing
ex 1002 00 00	Rye other than seed
1003 00 90	Barley other than seed
1004 40 90	Oats other than seed
1005 90 00	Maize (corn) other than seed
1007 00 90	Grain sorghum, other than hybrids for sowing
ex 1008 10 00	Buckwheat other than seed
ex 1008 20 00	Millet other than seed
ex 1008 90 10	Triticale other than seed
ex 1008 90 90	Other cereals other than seed
1201 00 90	Soya beans other than for sowing
1202 20 00	Shelled ground nuts
ex 1204 00 90	Linseed other than for sowing but destined for uses other than textiles
ex 1205 00 90	Rape or colza seeds other than for sowing (only those types referred to in Article 3(1)(a), (b) and (c) of Commission

---

1   There is a separate support system where the crop if grown other than on set aside land
     – see Commission Regulations 1308/70 and 619/71.
2   Article 4 of Commission Regulation 334/93.
3   Article 1 of Commission Regulation 334/93.
4   Annex II of Commission Regulation 334/93.
5   Annex 1 of Commission Regulation 334/93.

	Regulation (EEC) No. 2294/92
1206 00 90	Sunflower seeds other than for sowing
1207 20 90	Cotton seeds other than for sowing (only for 1993/94 harvest)
1207 30 90	Castor oil seeds other than for sowing
1207 40 90	Sesamum seeds other than for sowing
1207 50 90	Mustard seeds other than for sowing
1207 60 90	Safflower seeds other than for sowing
ex 1207 99 91	Hemp seeds other than for sowing and mentioned in Annex B of Commission Regulation (EEC) No. 1164/89 destined for uses other than textiles
1207 99 99	Other oil seeds and oleaginous fruits other than for sowing
ex 1209 29	Bitter lupin
ex 1211	Plants and parts of plants (including seeds and fruits), of a kind used primarily in perfumery, in pharmacy or for insecticidal, fungicidal or similar purposes, other than lavender, lavandin and sage
Chapter 14	Vegetable plaiting, stuffing or padding materials, or those used in brooms or brushes, vegetable products not elsewhere specified or included (eg. Broomcorn (Sorghum vulgare var. technicum))

Obviously short-rotation forest trees having a maximum period of 10 years and outdoor perennial plants will only be capable of cultivation if the non-rotational set-aside scheme is introduced.

It is only permissible to grow these raw materials if they are intended for use in the following end products:[1]

All products of the combined nomenclature:

(a) With the exception of:
- all of the products falling within chapters 1 to 24 of the combined nomenclature with the exception of:
- all products falling within CN chapter 15 which are intended for uses other than for human or animal consumption
- CN code 2207 20 00, for direct use in motor fuel or for processing for use in motor fuel

(b) with the inclusion of:
- all agricultural products set out in Annex I and their derivatives obtained by an intermediate transforming process which are burned in power stations for energy
- all products mentioned in Council Regulations (EEC) No. 1009/86 and (EEC) No 1010/86 on the condition that they are not obtained from cereals or potatoes cultivated on set-aside land and/or they do not contain products derived from cereals or potatoes cultivated on set-aside land.

In summary, what this means is that provided the value of the non-food products obtained from the processed raw materials is greater than the total value of any food products destined for animal or human consumption then these crops may be grown.[2]

---

1 Annex II of Commission Regulation 334/93.
2 Articles 3 and 8(3) of Commission Regulation 334/93.

Again, in non-legal terms, the permitted end uses are:

- oils, fats and waxes for uses other than human or animal consumption (oils sold as food supplements such as borage oil capsules will not be an acceptable end use)
- denatured ethyl alcohol and other spirits for direct use in motor fuel or for processing for use in motor fuel
- all the agricultural products contained in Annex I of 334/93 and their derivatives obtained by an intermediate transforming process which are then burned in power stations for energy
- all other end uses excluding products eligible for starch or sugar production refund and limited agricultural type products such as food products, seeds, live trees and other plants, bulbs, tubers, cut flowers, ornamentals, malt, starches, inulin and gluten. This list is not comprehensive.

6.9   Non-food crop rules

Having worked out whether growing a permitted raw material for a permitted end use with a correct economic valuation the claimant has to enter into a specific form of contract and submit it to the competent authority before the raw material is sown.[1]

The following rules apply:

- the claimant has to deliver all the raw material harvested to either the collector or first processor[2]
- the collector or first processor has to take delivery of it[3]
- the collector or first processor has to guarantee that an equivalent quantity of this raw material is used within the EEC in manufacturing one of the permitted end products[4]
- before first sowing the claimant has to submit to the competent authority a copy of the contract concluded between him and either the collector or the first processor. It has to be submitted by the claimant and it has to be signed prior to first sowing.[5]

The contract also has to contain:[6]

(a) the name and address of all of the contracting parties
(b) agreement as to the duration of the contract
(c) a description of the land involved giving details of the area, location

---

1 Article 6 of Commission Regulation 334/93.
2 Article 3.3 of Commission Regulation 334/93.
3 Article 3 of Commission Regulation 334/93.
4 Article 3.3 of Commission Regulation 334/93.
5 Article 6.1 of Commission Regulation 334/93. There is a limited exception for 1993 up to May 15 1993.
6 For hemp and flax the express terms are dealt with in Article 3 of Council Regulation 620/71 and Article 6 of Commission Regulation 334/93 but note also potential implied terms from Article 1 of Council Regulation 1215/71

and identity

(d) the species and variety of the raw material to be grown identifying any variations by reference to each parcel of land concerned

(e) the forecast quantity on harvest for each species/variety. The calculation of that forecast has to accord with guidance from the competent authority and the stated average yield for that species/variety for the region concerned. The contract also has to state the conditions relating to its delivery.

(f) an undertaking to comply with the obligation that the claimant must deliver and either the collector or the first processor must take delivery of the full amount of the harvest[1]

(g) agreement as to the principal end use envisaged for the raw material[2]

Member States may decide to implement a provision limiting a claimant to one contract for each raw material. Raw material is presumably limited to species as opposed to variety.[3]

In his annual area aid application[4] the claimant has to identify the land where raw materials are being grown and set out the species and varieties being grown together with the forecast yields for each species and variety.[5]

If for any reason the claimant finds that he is unable to provide the raw material – for example a crop failure – a contract can be adjusted or annulled.[6] In these circumstances to maintain his right to compensation the claimant has to return the land to fallow.

The claimant has to declare to his competent authority the amount of raw material harvested by species and variety and confirm to whom he has delivered the raw materials.[7] A special form is available for this purpose. In the case of crops eligible for intervention the quantity delivered may not be less than the forecast quantity.[8]

6.10   Economics of non-food crops

The main contracts available on any scale to arable farmers for the 1992/93 growing season have been:

- High erucic acid rape (HEAR) (for bio-fuel use)
- Double zero rapeseed (for use as industrial lubricants)
- Linseed

Compared to ordinary set-aside, where the same set-aside area payment is available but with very few costs, the economics of non-food crops on

---

1 Article 3.3 of Commission Regulation 334/93.
2 In compliance with Articles 3.1 and 8.3 of Commission Regulation 334/93.
3 Article 6.3 of Commission Regulation 334/93.
4 See the IACS Form.
5 Article 7.1 of Commission Regulation 334/93.
6 Article 7.2 of Commission Regulation 334/93.
7 Article 7.3 of Commission Regulation 334/93.
8 Para 45 in Annex 2 of IACS 1.

set-aside land do not generally look attractive. Typically the prices offered for industrial use crops have been at up to a 40% discount on the market price for the same or similar crops grown on other land. Thus linseed output might be budgeted at best at 2 tonnes per ha at £80 per tonne = £160 per ha (£64 per acre). At this level, the output barely covers the variable costs (seed, fertiliser, sprays) and certainly leaves very little to cover labour and machinery costs associated with growing, harvesting and handling the crop, not to mention the additional paperwork and management time satisfying inspectors that the crop on set-aside land has not been muddled with the same variety grown under the arable area scheme. The same situation can apply to spring double zero rapeseed, where the output levels are likely to be around £160 – £200 per ha, although there is probably a higher potential than with linseed.

Non-food crops are not without their problems, for example a 100 m separation distance must be maintained between winter double zero rapeseed and winter high erucic acid rapeseed – although this has been waived for crops sown before September 30 1992. Also a 100 m separation must be observed between spring double zero rapeseed and spring high erucic acid rapeseed.

However, in situations where there is genuine spare capacity in labour and machinery, and perhaps where land is preferred to be kept in cultivation (possibly because of a weed problem), the growing of non-food crops has a place and useful experience will be gained. There is clearly further potential to develop non-food crops in the UK with a much higher proportion of land going into set-aside than in most other parts of Europe.

6.11   Payment

Payment of the set-aside area compensatory payment[1] can be made before the raw material is processed, but cannot be made before the raw material has been delivered to the collector or first processor.[2] Additionally, before payment can be made:[3]

- the claimant must have made his declarations referred to in the previous paragraph
- the collector or first processor must have deposited a copy of the contract of the competent authority within 20 working days of the conclusion of the contract[4]
- the competent authority must have checked to satisfy itself that the contract relates to a permitted raw material for a permitted end use.[5] In doing this the competent authority has to check the value of non-

---

1 Article 7 of Council Regulation 1765/92.
2 Article 7.4 of Commission Regulation 334/93.
3 Article 7.4 of Commission Regulation 334/93.
4 Article 8.1 of Commission Regulation 334/93.
5 Article 8.2 of Commission Regulation 334/93.

food products against products for human or animal consumption[1]
- the competent authority has to have received proof that the full amount of a security, being 120% of the value of the area compensatory payment,[2] has been lodged by either the collector or first processor with the competent authority.[3]
  At least 50% of the security must have been lodged within 20 days of the signed contract with the claimant and the balance within 20 days of receipt of the raw material.[4]
- the competent authority must have checked that the contract between claimant and either collector or first processor contained all the appropriate terms.[5]

Therefore, assuming that the collector or first processor is not likely to deposit the second half of the security before he has to (within 20 days of receiving the raw material) and bearing in mind all the checks that have to be made the claimant is unlikely to receive the area compensatory payment for some time after delivering the raw material.

Delivery of the raw material triggers another obligation on the collector or first processor which is to inform the competent authority within 20 days of the quantity of raw material received. Also he has to specify the species and variety of the raw material as well as the name and address of the contracting party and the place of delivery.[6] The collector has the additional burden of having to inform the competent authority of the name and address of the consignee, the first processor/buyer of the raw material[7] within three months of receiving the raw material. All the intermediaries have to be notified by the collector to the competent authority[8] and they in turn have to notify the competent authority of the name and address of whoever they sell the raw material to.[9]

The security itself is released back to the collector or first processor on a pro rata basis as and when the competent authority are satisfied that the raw material has been legitimately processed.[10] The processing has to take place within three years of delivery of the raw material.[11] There are detailed rules relating to movement of raw materials between Member States.[12] By now it will have been noted that dealing in raw material produced on set-aside land is a pastime suitable only for those able to keep good records and with efficient management systems. Member States have to specify the records which collectors and first

---

1 Article 8.3 of Commission Regulation 334/93.
2 Article 9.2 of Commission Regulation 334/93.
3 Article 9.1 of Commission Regulation 334/93.
4 Article 9.1 of Commission Regulation 334/93.
5 See Article 6.1 of Commission Regulation 334/93 referred to above.
6 Article 8.4(a) of Commission Regulation 334/93.
7 Article 8.4(b) of Commission Regulation 334/93.
8 Article 8.4(c) of Commission Regulation 334/93.
9 Article 8.4(c) of Commission Regulation 334/93.
10 Article 9.2 of Commission Regulation 334/93.
11 Article 10.2 of Commission Regulation 334/93.
12 Articles 8.4(e) and 9.3 and 10 of Commission Regulation 334/93.

processors keep.

The minimum level of records required of a collector[1] are:

- the quantities of all raw materials bought and sold for processing
- the name and address of subsequent buyers/processors.

The minimum level of records required of the first processor[2] *on a daily basis* are:

- the quantities of all raw materials purchased for processing
- the quantities of raw materials processed, together with quantities and types of end products, co-products and by-products obtained from them
- wastage during processing losses
- the quantities destroyed and the justification for such action
- the quantities and types of product sold or given away by the processor and the prices obtained
- the name and address of subsequent buyers/processors.

To round it all off the competent authority is obliged to carry out controls including physical checks, inspection of commercial documents and consistency between the level of raw products delivered and volume of end products by reference to technical processing co-efficients.[3]

These controls have to cover at least 10% of the processing operations taking place and are to be selected on the basis of risk analysis.[4]

If problems with compliance are detected by the competent authority it is required to step up checks and inform the Commission.[5]

6.12   Minimum size

Parcels of set-aside land have to cover a minimum area of 0.3 contiguous hectares and have a width of at least 20 m.[6] Smaller areas can only be considered if they involve whole fields with permanent boundaries such as walls, hedges or watercourses.[7]

When planning set-aside producers should bear in mind that although small strips are allowed, this could cause problems in later years if the producer remains in rotational set-aside because of the six-year rule.

6.13   Declarations

Producers submit an annual declaration form[8] which it is anticipated will

---

1   Article 11.1(a) of Commission Regulation 334/93.
2   Article 11.1(b) of Commission Regulation 334/93.
3   Article 11.2 of Commission Regulation 334/93.
4   Article 11.2 of Commission Regulation 334/93.
5   Article 11.3 of Commission Regulation 334/93.
6   Article 3.1 of Commission Regulation 2293/92.
7   Article 3.1 of Commission Regulation 2293/92.
8   Article 4.2 of Commission Regulation 2293/92.

set out areas for set-aside and areas for arable crops. Each producer has to submit a single set-aside declaration which will be broken down by region.[1] The general rule is that those applying for arable area payments under the general scheme and who farm in more than one yield region (quite common in Scotland with so called "split units", part in LFA and part in non-LFA), must set-aside 15% in each yield region. There are now two exceptions to this general rule:

(i) if the set-aside commitment in one of the regions is less than 2 ha (ie claiming on less than 11.33 ha of crops), then the 2 ha or less can be set-aside in another yield region.

(ii) if the land actually adjoins and straddles the border between two yield regions, the land within that block can be counted against land within the same block but the other side of the border.

In these situations payment for set-aside will be at the rate appropriate to the region in which the set-aside is actually situated. These exceptions may not apply to non-rotational set-aside to be introduced in 1993/4.

The interpretation of what is intended by "a single application" has changed since the publication of MAFF's original explanatory booklet (AR2) and the IACS 1 booklet. Originally it was indicated that a business with several farms but with different farm managers could submit separate applications by each farm manager.[2]

In the IACS 1 booklet there still appears to be some flexibility despite the statement "All your farms in the United Kingdom farmed as one unit should be the subject of a single area aid application".[3] Later, the booklet states that a separate application must be submitted in respect of each separate business[4] and evidence of more than one business would require "separate farm plans and accounts and independence of decision making". This does not appear to go as far as the Scottish IACS 1 booklet which is clear that separate applications can only be made where farms are run as "legally separate businesses" and goes on:

A separate business will have a separate business name and accounts, separate land and housing, substantially separate supplies of labour, machinery and feed, and will have been accepted by the Inland Revenue as separate for tax purposes.[5]

6.14 Inaccuracies

If the producer has set-aside less land than required then the following rules apply:

(i) providing the producer is within 1 ha of requirement if the set-aside

---

1 Article 4.2 of Commission Regulation 2293/92.
2 MAFF explanatory booklet para 76.
3 Para 14 IACS 1 (MAFF).
4 Para 134 IACS 1 (MAFF).
5 Para 11 IACS 1 (1993) (SOAFD).

requirement is 10 ha or more; or

(ii) providing the producer is within 10% of requirement if the set-aside requirement is less than 10 ha (so if 5 ha should have been set-aside, at least 4.5 ha must have actually been set-aside)

the producer will be paid on the actual area of land set-aside and the area payments will be reduced pro rata for each crop.[1]

This last clause "the area payment will be reduced pro rata" does imply a real penalty to a producer taking advantage of this tolerance of up to 1 ha, and a penalty which is not immediately obvious. Thus, if there are 100 ha in total and instead of setting aside 15 ha a producer sets aside 14 ha (perhaps because there is a field of this size) the payment will be made on the 14 ha plus 86 ha x 14/15ths ha of crops. The reduction will be spread across cereal, oil seeds and protein crops on a pro rata basis. Now 14/15ths is 93.3% so that the penalty is 6.7% over the whole 86 ha. This could be a substantial amount. The following shows the potential loss in 1993/94 from claiming the one hectare tolerance on a 100 ha English farm with 50% cereals and 25% each of oil seeds and proteins:

A. Set-aside exactly 15%   £
  Set-aside compensation   15 ha @ £261.7/ha   3,925
  Crop compensation   85 ha @ £282/ha   23,970
                               100 ha   27,895

B. Set-aside at 15% minus 1 ha
  Set-aside compensation   14 ha @ £261.7/ha   3,664
  Crop compensation   86 ha @ £282 x 14/15ths   22,635
                               100 ha   26,299

A-B = Loss of compensation =   1,596
  Less 1 ha gross margin extra in B   (500)
  Net penalty from claiming tolerance   1,096

This example shows the net penalty (after allowing for an extra one hectare of crops actually grown) to be about £1,100 in the 100 ha example. In fact the penalty is much the same whether the business is 100 ha or 1,000 ha because the tolerance is limited to 1 ha and in the 1,000 ha situation the calculation would be 149/150ths (99.3%) or a penalty of 0.7% over the 851 ha grown.

If the producer has set-aside more than he is required to do then if the set-aside requirement is 10 ha or more payment will be made on up to 1 ha extra. If the set-aside requirement is less than 10 ha then payment will be made on up to 10% over requirement.

---

1 Article 5 of Commission Regulation 2293/92 which may be amended by a further regulation incresing the tolerance to 15% of the requirement. MAFF's view is that this provision applies when the inaccuracy arises because the farmer did not understand how to do the calculation. Contrast with the provision of Article 9 of Comission Regulation 3887/92.

So if the requirement is 5 ha but more has been set-aside then the producer may be paid on up to 5.5 ha (5 plus 10%) in total.[1]

---

1 Article 5.1 of Commission Regulation 2293/92.

Land transfers

7   A crucial question is what happens to area aid payments when land is transferred. Any change of occupation by farming businesses whether by sale, lease or transfer by inheritance is likely to raise questions as to who is entitled to receive the arable area payments for the year concerned. Possibly recognising that legislating on what should happen when land is transferred was too big a task even for the European Community, no legislation has been put in place on this subject although the European Commission have introduced guidelines. The guidelines basically provide for freedom of contract between the parties, but only if the land is transferred before May 15. If the transfer takes place after May 15 then the arable area payments are made to the person submitting a valid application before May 15.

If a transfer takes place before May 15 either party can apply so long as the applicant has been in occupation of all the land at some time during the cropping/set-aside year. If the new occupier claims and receives the area aid he must ensure that:

(a) the previous occupier has the correct set-aside and has followed all the management rules, and

(b) that he is able to meet all the requirements (for example the applicant must have farmed the set-aside land for two years before it can be eligible, unless he falls into one of the exemption categories). In many ways it may be better for the new occupier to be the applicant as he will have every incentive to comply with all the rules or conditions. Whatever situation applies it is in the interests of the applicant to make sure that the other party has or will comply with all the rules and this will require careful legal documentation.

The real complications of transfers occur when parcels of land in respect of which applications have been made are transferred in parts. Each application under the main scheme has to maintain the correct ratio of set-aside to relevant arable crops. In this situation it would seem that only the original occupier can sensibly make the application, and thus he has to try to ensure that all new occupiers maintain any set-aside strictly to the rules. This could be tricky where for example a block of land had been sold which was in grass set-aside, and the new occupier wanted to use it for his own horses or other livestock. If at all possible it would be best to avoid land transfers during the set-aside period, December 15 to July 15.

Taxation

8   Area aid payments will form part of the trading receipts of the farming business and will be taken into account in computing the trading profit brought into account for income or corporation tax. The time at which such aid should be brought into account for tax is a difficult area. Much will depend upon correct accounting practice and it is possible to have more than one correct accounting treatment depending upon the particular facts and circumstances of the case. The most important factor is the purpose of the grant. Where a grant is made to meet particular costs then it would be correct to match it with those costs and reduce them accordingly. If those costs are included in the closing stock valuation then the Revenue are likely to accept that the cost figure used should be the net cost after deducting the grant. On the other hand if the grant is made to subsidise the proceeds from sale of the specific crop rather than to meet particular costs the correct treatment would be to recognise the grant as income in the year in which that crop is sold. The Inland Revenue have treated aid under the Oil Seeds Support Scheme 1992 as a subsidy towards the selling price and the likelihood is that this is the correct approach to other area compensatory payments.

The Revenue have not yet given any guidance on area payments for cereals and proteins and the requirements of those schemes do differ from the requirements under the Oil Seeds Support Scheme. There is, for example no requirement to harvest a cereal crop in order to qualify for area payment. None the less all the schemes require the crop to be sown and grown, and it is probably safer to treat the grant in each case as having more of the nature of a subsidy towards sale proceeds than to meet particular costs. Thus accounts which recognise the payments as income at the time a crop is sold should be accepted for tax purposes. Until then payments received should normally be shown as deferred income on the balance sheet.

The farming consequences

9   Background

It would be fair to say that the arable farmer in the UK is far happier with the reality of CAP Reform in the Spring of 1993 than he was with its prospect some two years earlier. While this has much to do with a potential short-term financial windfall brought about by successive green pound devaluations, *viz*

- September 16 1992   1 ECU = £0.795423
- March 1 1993   1 ECU = £0.980715

it also reflects significant compromise of the original reform proposals. The key issue is the compensation of set-aside.

Under the proposals first put forward in spring 1991 by the then European Agriculture Commissioner, Ray MacSharry, set-aside was marked at 15%, with only the first 6 ha in England being compensated. Therefore any farmer with over 40 ha of eligible crops joining the scheme and setting aside his full complement would have part of his arable land (ie his set-aside area of over 6 ha) producing no income whatsoever. For the larger farmer, in particular, the consequences for profit were potentially devastating.

Consider the possible impact of these original proposals on two arable farms growing all eligible crops, one of 40 ha and one of 800 ha, by reference to possible changes in farm gross margin. The gross margin is calculated as:

Total Output minus Direct (Variable) Costs

Output includes crop sales and area payments, while the main variable costs for arable crops are seeds, fertilisers and sprays. Potential gross margin for these two farms pre- and post-reform might have been as follows:

Comparison reduction in total farm gross margin if only 6 ha of set-aside compensated as per original proposals

	40 ha farm £	800 ha farm £
Pre-cap reform		
Total farm gross margin	22,000	440,000
Post-original reform proposals		
Total farm gross margin	20,270	375,570
Variance + (−)	(1,730)	(64,430)
	= (7.86%)	= (14.64)%

(Assumes 1 ECU = £0.980715, set-aside = £261.70/ha)

In a well-managed farm business a reasonable target for profit would be 25% of total farm gross margin. In our two examples target profit prior to reform would therefore have been:

	40 ha farm £	800 ha farm £
Pre-cap reform		
Total farm gross margin	22,000	440,000
Farm target profit	5,500	110,000

The central problem for the arable farmer is that with set-aside at 15% the reforms do not enable pro-rata savings in fixed (or overhead) costs to be made, although marginal savings in some categories (eg fuel, machinery repairs) are possible. Reduced gross margins therefore directly affect profit, so for our two farms:

	40 ha farm £	800 ha farm £
Target profit pre-reform	5,500	110,000
Reform gross margin reduction	1,730	64,430
Potential profit post reform	3,770	45,570

Without fixed cost savings this represents a 31% reduction in profit for the 40 ha farmer and a dramatic 58% for his 800 ha counterpart.

No wonder in the UK, with high average farm size, there was an outcry from the arable farming lobby.

In the final analysis what the Agricultural Ministers agreed in late May 1992, in a spate of "five to midnight" compromise, was an arable reform package with full set-aside compensation along with a host of other more minor but none the less important concessions (not least on the possible treatments of set-aside land). The UK arable farmer rightly breathed a long sigh of relief.

Who is affected?

While the introduction of compensation for the entire set-aside area removed the main discrepancy between the smaller and larger arable farmers, it became apparent that the financial consequences of the final package would vary between farms, particularly according to soil quality and the farmers' technical ability. In general it seemed that those least affected would be the less effective operators on the poorer soil types.

By way of illustration consider a 200 ha farm growing all combinable crops. Before the reforms the rotation (or cropping sequence) was the commonly-used four-course of:

- winter wheat
- oil seed rape
- winter wheat
- beans

Annual cropping was therefore:

winter wheat	=	100 ha
oil seed rape	=	50 ha
beans	=	50 ha

Assuming that set-aside replaced part of the break crop acreage (thereby maintaining the full area of wheat, often the most profitable crop on farms of this type) the post-reform cropping might be:

winter wheat	=	100 ha
oil seed rape	=	35 ha
beans	=	35 ha
set-aside	=	30 ha

The following table sets out the gross margin for this farm, both before and after reform, at three levels of yield performance – "low", "medium" and "high". The example is calculated at the March 1 1993 exchange rate of 1 ECU = £0.980715.

CAP arable reform: example pre and post reform
gross margins 1991 and 1993 harvest (England)
1 ECU = £0.980715

Yield performance	Low	Medium	High
Winter wheat – feed (T/ha)	6.00	7.30	8.60
Winter oil seed rape (T/ha)	2.50	3.00	3.50
Winter beans (T/ha)	2.70	3.45	4.20
Pre cap reform (1991)			
Total farm gross margin	£75,425	£100,738	£126,050
Post cap reform (1993)			
Total farm gross margin	£103,202	£121,927	£140,652
Variance +(-)	£27,777	£21,189	£14,602
	= 36.8%	= 21.0%	= 11.5%

Two striking features emerge:

- relatively, the poorer performer is better off
- the gross margin at all three levels of performance improves as a result of the reforms.

It is interesting to repeat the calculation using the exchange rate that applied until mid-September 1992, that was 1 ECU = £0.795423: see table at top of p 57.

Comparatively the poorer performer is still better off, his gross margin in fact increasing. For the medium and, most markedly, high performers, however, gross margins decline, a salutary reminder to all those lulled by the apparent benefits of successive green pound devaluations.

The relative effect of the reforms should not mask the fact that in absolute terms the better performers still remain significantly better off than their poorer counterparts, even if the gap between the two might have diminished.

**CAP arable reform: example pre and post reform
gross margins 1991 and 1993 harvest (England)
1 ECU = £0.795423**

Yield performance	Low	Medium	High
Winter wheat – feed (T/ha)	6.00	7.30	8.60
Winter oil seed rape (T/ha)	2.50	3.00	3.50
Winter beans (T/ha)	2.70	3.45	4.20

Pre cap reform (1991)

Total farm gross margin	£75,425	£100,738	£126,050

Post cap reform (1993)

Total farm gross margin	£83,875	£100,513	£117,150
Variance +(-)	£8,450	(£225)	(£8,900)
	= 11.2%	= (0.2%)	= (7.0%)

That this is the case is a consequence of moving from a policy of supporting prices, which inevitably favours those who produce most, to one where the crop itself forms only part of total output.

The balance of support

If we compare the low and high performers of the above example then for 1993 assuming:

- 1 ECU = £0.980715
- Feed wheat price = £105/tonne (ex-farm)
- Oil seed rape price = £140/tonne (ex-farm)
- Bean price = £100/tonne (ex-farm)

the area payment in the English yield region represents a proportion of the total output of each crop as follows:

Winter wheat	Low	High
Crop output £/ha	630.00	903.00
Area payment £/ha	145.39	145.39
Total output	775.39	1,048.39
Area payment as % Total output	18.75	13.87

Oilseed rape	Low	High
Crop output £/ha	350.00	490.00
Area payment £/ha	459.49	459.49
Total output £/ha	809.49	949.49
Area payment as % Total output	56.57	48.39

Beans	Low	High
Crop output £/ha	270.00	420.00
Area payment £/ha	378.02	378.02
Total output £/ha	648.02	798.02
Area payment as % Total output	58.33	47.37

With the removal of the price support the area support for both oilseeds and pulses (which remains unchanged throughout 1993–1995 transitional period) forms such a significant proportion of gross output that it makes no financial sense growing these crops without matching set-aside and area payments.

Area payments for cereals, however, are introduced on a staged basis through the three year transitional period, with intervention prices declining.

Cereal area payments/intervention – England

Harvest year	1993	1994	1995
Area payment (£/ha)	145.39	203.55	261.70
Intervention[1] (£/T – November)	114.63	105.92	98.17

As a result the case for winter wheat in this first transitional year is not quite so straightforward. As it is possible to "mix and match" set-aside and area payment claims many in the autumn of 1992 were asking the question:

> While I intend to set-aside an area so that I can claim area payments on my break crops, would I be better off by
> • planting the whole of the balance to wheat with no set-aside, thereby losing no cropping area but foregoing the cereal area payments
> or
> • setting aside sufficient hectares so that area payment could be claimed on the entire wheat crop?

In the event an exceptionally wet autumn provided a simple and clear answer. Many crops remained undrilled while others failed, with the result that wheat hectarage dropped by default on many holdings.

It is however interesting to speculate what the answer to the question might have been if drilling the whole area to wheat had been a practical possibility, knowing what in the spring of 1993 we do about our exit from the ERM, the devaluation of the green pound and its affect on area payments and commodity prices. Putting aside potential fixed cost savings and any complications that might arise with rotations, it is possible to calculate the wheat yield that would be required in order to justify not setting aside and making area claims. To demonstrate this consider the farmer growing only winter wheat, assuming that:

- 1 ECU = £0.980715
- ex-farm price for wheat is £105 per tonne
- wheat area payment is £145.39 per ha
- set-aside payment is £261.07 per ha

On this basis wheat yield would need to exceed 12.43 tonnes per ha (5.03 tonnes per acre) for the farmer to be better off by not setting land aside, ie if the average wheat yield is below this figure, farm gross

---

1 Assuming application of the reducing coefficient.

margin declines. This level of performance is only achievable by the technically outstanding on the very best soil types.

If we re-work the calculation for the 1995 harvest, assuming:

- 1 ECU = £0.980715
- ex-farm price for wheat is £90 per tonne
- wheat area payment is £261.70 per ha
- set-aside remains at 15% and payment is £261.70 per ha

the break-even yield increases to 21.83 tonnes per ha (8.84 tonnes per acre) – well beyond commercial reality.

While the balance of financial support varies between the eligible crops, the reforms introduced for the transitional period (1993, 1994 and 1995 harvests) are so structured that for most farmers set-aside is an almost inevitable choice. This of course could well change if area payments decline and the requirement to set-aside increases.

Arable planning for the reforms

In practice incorporating set-aside into arable farming is nothing like as simple as the financial theory suggests. Arable farming systems which include non-eligible crops (eg potatoes, sugar beet) may find the planning exercise somewhat easier than those with 100% eligible crops, for whom the questions can be a thorny one.

In order to accommodate set-aside and the reform measures the main factors that farmers will take into account will be:

- crop rotations
- crop gross margins
- labour and machinery costs

Crop rotations

Theoretically farm profits are best served by removing poorer perform-ing crops to accommodate set-aside, although this may not be fully achievable in practice if rotational plans are to be broadly maintained. Nine months of canvassing farmer meetings suggests that these are most frequently winter barley, second wheat crops and oil seed rape.

Rotational set-aside, set at one year in six, may play havoc with existing cropping plans. Additionally current amendments to rotations may need further rethinking if there are future changes to the set-aside percentage.

Many see set-aside as potentially a new "break crop" in rotations. There is little doubt that the cheapest and therefore, for many, preferred option will be natural regeneration of cereal stubble followed by Summer fallow. With the wet conditions of Autumn 1992 this was the only practical option for many. The fallow option after May 1 will allow weed control, and cultivations which will help both weed control and soil structure as well as providing timely cultivations for the following crop. Whether this option will give a sufficient disease break if the following crop is to be winter wheat (particularly for diseases such as Take-all) is unclear, with professional opinion divided. As a result some are considering following set-aside with the early drilled winter oil seed rape which, in terms of timing, is the crop most likely to benefit from the Summer fallow cultivations and which will not be affected by cereal disease carry-over. Alternatively the autumn establishment of an oats/brassica green cover crop on set-aside (eg oats/oil seed rape) may provide a more genuine break before a following wheat crop.

Gross margins

One of the central criteria of the reforms is the reduction of commodity prices which inevitably must change the cost-effectiveness of certain inputs. This was well shown with the 1992 oil seed rape crop when, in response to a halving of the rape price, farms frequently reduced their use of nitrogen fertiliser by 15% – 30%.

Such a shift in cost-effectiveness, without matching changes in input prices, is illustrated by the break-even yield required to make a bean fungicide cost-effective, before and after reform:

Example – fungicide on field beans

Disease – Chocolate Spot
Break-even yield per ha

	Beans @ £160/tonne	Beans @ £90/tonne
Fungicide cost	£23.52	£23.52
Break-even yield	0.15T/ha	0.26T/ha

It is difficult in 1993, with the price distortions arising from green pound devaluations, to detect any change in farmer practice. Indeed future opportunities for savings in variable costs may not be as great as many may think, although there may well be an adjustment, particularly of some spray chemical prices, in response to revised crop values.

There is no doubt that the reforms by removing a part of the national arable area and reducing prices, have dealt a potentially major blow to the manufacturers and distributors of fertilisers and agrochemicals.

Some farmers are seeking to mitigate the effect of set-aside on farm gross margin by growing industrial crops on the set-aside areas although the gross margin premium may not be great.

Consider the comparative gross margins of High Erucic Acid Oil Seed Rape (HEAR) and set-aside: see table on p 61.
The extra gross margin of £35.50 per ha is unlikely to cover the extra fixed costs associated with growing, harvesting and handling of this crop.

Labour and machinery costs

A central problem with set-aside at 15% is that pro-rata economies in labour and machinery costs are difficult to achieve, with the inevitable consequence that unit costs on the cropped area increase.

Comparison of gross margin performance of high erucic acid oil seed rape (HEAR) on set-aside with ordinary set-aside (England)
1 ECU = £0.980715

	HEAR on set-aside £/ha	£/ha	Ordinary set-aside £/ha	£/ha
Output				
2.5 T/ha @ £95.00/T	237.50		Nil	
Set-aside area payment	261.70		261.70	
Total gross output		499.20		261.70
Variable costs				
Seed	30.00		Nil	
Fertiliser	86.00		Nil	
Spray	86.00		Nil	
Total variable costs		202.00		Nil
Gross margin		297.20		261.70

Savings are most likely for costs such as fuel, machinery repairs and casual labour, while in other categories – eg full time labour, machinery depreciation – economies are likely to be more difficult with set-aside at 15%.

One opportunity that the reforms may provide is to reduce the "autumn work peak", the disproportionate workload that many arable farms suffer in the July – October period. Frequently such a peak provides the justification for excessive overhead costs. With the reduced crop area that results from set-aside and the opportunity, on some soil types, to reintroduce spring cropping, work loads can be more evenly distributed and costs reduced.

Furthermore, where spring crops are an appropriate alternative (promoted by the introduction of area payments) crop establishment costs may well be lower as the following example for oil seed rape shows:

Oil seed rape establishment costs – typical contract rates

	Winter (£/ha)	Spring (£/ha)
3 x heavy disc	96.00	
Roll	16.50	
Drill	20.00	
Roll	16.50	
Plough and press		50.00
Power harrow		33.00
Drill		20.00
Roll		16.50
Total cost	149.00	119.50
Potential saving		29.50

The alternative to cost-cutting is through expansion of farmed area, to maintain or even reduce unit labour and machinery costs. This is particularly relevant where reductions in full-time staff are difficult if not impossible.

To draw together these three main factors – that is rotations, gross margins and labour and machinery costs – let us look once against at our 200 ha farmer growing wheat, oil seed rape and beans, and see what sort of practical changes might be made in response to the reforms.

Rotation   include set-aside as break crop – reduce oil seed rape/beans acreages equally – "four course" becomes "six course", ie winter wheat/oil seed rape/winter wheat/beans/winter wheat/set-aside. If weather allows in autumn 1993 plant oats/brassica cover for set-aside with aim of providing better break.

Gross margins   maintain area of key cash crop – wheat. Look for economies in variable costs including greater use of home-saved seed and reduced nitrogen fertiliser use on oil seed rape – further changes in fertilisers/sprays depend on crop value.

Labour and machinery   retain full-time employment, but reduce casual labour. Plan longer machinery life (lower depreciation) reduced fuel costs and savings in machinery repairs, including costs associated with the storage and marketing of smaller physical quantities of crop.

Future developments

The arable regime is likely to be constantly under review. Linseed will be incorporated as an eligible crop in 1994, probably with its own set-aside.

Oil seed rape will be affected by the EEC/US Agreement and as this starts in 1994, so autumn 1993 plantings will be influenced.

Non-rotational set-aside proposals are awaited by July 1993. Of particular interest will be the opportunities for short-rotation coppice on non-rotational set-aside land.

Further developments of non-food crops on set-aside land may also occur.

The set-aside percentage may also change – upwards seeming to be the only likely course, although to what level is difficult to assess.

Future management of set-aside may well change, possibly effecting rotational considerations. Of particular importance is the position of grass as a green cover crop and the ability to make use of the cover outside the seven-month set-aside period.

Unquestionably the future holds continuing change. This makes forward planning difficult for farmers, particularly for crop rotations, and means that thinking will need to be continually revised. Traditional husbandry practices may on occasion be sacrificed at the altar of maximum area support. The successful arable farmer will be "light on his feet", responding rapidly to detailed changes in policy.

Conclusions

Anticipating the 1993 potential financial Indian Summer masks the consequences of the reform of the Common Agricultural Policy for arable farmers in the UK.

There is nothing to suggest in the medium to longer term that the underlying decline in the potential profitability from UK arable farming in the United Kingdom will not continue. This would clearly be significantly accelerated by higher requirements for set-aside and a strengthening in the value of the pound.

The prudent farmer will be looking to create real reductions in costs of production, either through savings or by an increase in farmed area and will prepare for the likely real reductions in the gross margin potential of the holding.

D. BEEF

The common market in beef and veal

10   The common organisation in the market in beef and veal was established in 1968.[1] Until the reforms with which this book deals were implemented the EC system was based on price support mechanisms aimed at keeping prices within the Community at an agreed level. The chosen mechanisms were support buying and private storage coupled with levies on imports from outside the EC and export refunds when beef was exported outside the EC.

There are three key prices for the beef and veal regime. These are the guide price, intervention price and reference price. For the year 1992/93 these were fixed at:

Guide price	200	ECUs per 100 kg live weight
Intervention price	343	ECUs per 100 kg deadweight

The guide price is akin to the target price in cereals and is the price which it is considered desirable for producers within the Community to obtain under normal market conditions. It is fixed annually for the year commencing on the first Monday in April but for 1993 the marketing year has been extended to July.

The intervention price is fixed on a deadweight basis and is set for a marketing year. For 1992/93 the intervention price was set at 343 ECUs per 100 kg deadweight for steer and young bull carcasses classified under the EC classification system as R3. There are numerous variables for different grades. It will be reduced by 5% for 1993/94.

The reference price moves because it is an attempt to measure the EC market price for fat cattle. Prices in each Member State are monitored and balanced to give a weighted average of cattle prices across the Community. The price is calculated weekly and when the reference price falls below the guide price this is an indication that steps may need to be taken to strengthen the market and vice versa.

Central to the reform of the CAP in the beef sector is an overhaul of intervention.[2] A substantial reduction in intervention prices and amounts brought into intervention has been determined as the way ahead. Under the intervention system the intervention agency in any Member State is obliged to purchase, when market conditions reach a given state, specified categories of beef at a fixed price.

The amounts bought into intervention from 1988 onwards are set out below:

	Tonnes
1988	390,728
1989	152,219
1990	657,462
1991	1,027,434
1992	851,868

---

1 Council Regulation 805/68.
2 Council Regulation 1302/73 and Commission Regulations 2226/78 and 859/89.

Under the reforms, the prices paid for intervention will be reduced by 15% over three years and reducing ceilings on the amount that may be purchased into intervention are imposed.

Also there is imposed a staggered reduction in the maximum weight limit of carcasses entering intervention.[1]

	maximum weight limit	
At present		420 kgs
July 1 1993		380 kgs
January 1 1994		360 kgs
July 1 1994		340 kgs

The beef special premium,[2] which replaced the variable premium scheme, has operated since 1989 as a direct subsidy to producers. The premium was paid at slaughter on a maximum of 90 male cattle per legally separate business per year. The rate of payment in 1992 was 40 ECU which, for much of the year, was worth £31.80, but rose to £35.90 in December, following the initial green pound devaluations. Under the reforms, the beef special premium is no longer claimed at slaughter, but is available twice in the animal's life with a maximum of 90 per business at each age group. Therefore the maximum per business is now extended 180. This extension of potential claims sits strangely against the need to control expenditure, and looks particularly inept when it is considered that the second claim is a virtual inducement to keep the animal longer and to a higher slaughter weight, therefore increasing the supply of beef. However, the late introduction of maximum carcase weights for intervention (only agreed by the Council of Ministers in December 1992 and amended in early 1993) seems to be a recognition of the potential problem the new regime was encouraging.

The new beef regime is full of contradictions. Another concerns the introduction of limits on the total numbers claimed in each Member State, thereby on the face of it restricting community expenditure to a predetermined level. These limits, or "regional reference numbers" operate in much the same way as the "regional base area" introduced under the arable regime. However, unlike the arable regime, the beef regime contains an open-ended element, which is the second claim. This is because the limits which are based on historic numbers will only be measured against future claims at the first age. All second age claims will, therefore, be additional to numbers claimed in the past. However, any scaling down of payments due to exceeding the regional reference number will apply to both age groups.

In 1992 approximately £44m was paid to beef producers in the UK under the beef special scheme. For 1993 the amount of the claim is set at £56.34 giving an estimated expenditure in the UK of approximately £70m. This figure of £70m is misleading in the sense that it is only the expenditure for that financial year and only involves payment of the

---

1 Article 4(2)9 of Commission Regulation 859/89 as amended by Commission Regulation 685/93.
2 Council Regulation 468/87 and Commission Regulations 859/87 and 714/89.

60% advance. Thus for the following year anticipated expenditure is very roughly of the order of £120m.

The suckler cow premium had operated since 1980[1] and is another form of direct aid to beef producers. Under the common agricultural policy reforms it is drastically reorganised with the imposition of individual ceilings across the community. The amount per claim is initially set at £65.73 per head in the UK. In 1992 the total premium payment in the UK amounted to more than £86m.

Lastly, a new system involving either a slaughter premium or lightweight intervention has been set up to deal with male calves of dairy breeds. The UK has opted for lightweight intervention.

---

1 Council Regulation 1357/80 as amended and Commission Regulation 1244/82 as amended.

Intervention

11.1 Reduction in intervention

A reducing maximum quantity of meat that may be brought into intervention is imposed for the whole community.[1]

	Tonnes
1993	750,000
1994	650,000
1995	550,000
1996	400,000
1997 onwards	350,000

The intervention price has to be set before the start of each marketing year[2] and for 1992/93 the marketing year has been extended to July 4 1993 and the 1993/94 marketing year commences on July 5 1993.[3]

Intervention can only take place in certain conditions[4] and must then operate under tender procedures aimed to ensure reasonable support of the market.[5]

Under the detailed classification procedure[6] quality groups of meat are identified. Tender procedures for each group may be opened when for two consecutive weeks both the average community grading market price is less than 84% of the intervention price and the average market price in the Member State or region is less than 80% of the intervention price. The tender arrangements are suspended if either for two consecutive weeks both the above conditions are not met or buying in is no longer appropriate for reasonable support of the market taking into account seasonal developments for slaughterings.[7]

There is a cushion on these potentially drastic reductions in the scope of intervention. Intervention is opened if for two consecutive weeks both the average community market price falls below 78% of the intervention price and the average market price in the Member State or region is less than 60% of the intervention price. All offers into intervention have to be accepted in those market conditions and quantities taken into intervention under this mechanism do not count as part of the maximum quantities for intervention.[8]

Under both the normal and cushion (or "safety net") intervention systems only offers less than or equal to the average Member State or regional market price, increased by an amount determined by objective

---

1 Article 6.1 of Council Regulation 805/68 as amended by Article 4(l) of Council Regulation 2066/92.
2 Article 6.2 of Council Regulation 805/68 as amended by Council Regulation 2066/92.
3 Article 1 of Council Regulation 660/93.
4 Articles 6.2 and 6.4 of Council Regulation 805/68 as amended by Council Regulation 2066/92.
5 Article 6.1 of Council Regulation 805/68 as amended by Council Regulation 2066/92.
6 Council Regulation 1208/81.
7 Article 6.3 of Council Regulation 805/68 as amended by Council Regulation 2066/92.
8 Article 6.4 of Council Regulation 805/68 as amended by Council Regulation 2066/92.

criteria,[1] can be accepted.

Tender procedures have to be fair to ensure equality of access to all persons concerned.[2]

11.2   Lightweight intervention

Member States have the option of introducing a slaughter premium of 100 ECUs per male dairy breed calf withdrawn from production before the age of 10 days. Payment under the scheme must be made within 4 months of the application being submitted.[3] Member States had the alternative of introducing a lightweight intervention scheme and the UK has opted to do this. These special intervention measures are permitted from January 1 1993 to December 31 1995.[4] However, these quantities do count towards the Community's ceilings for intervention.[5]

Lightweight intervention is not expected to be significant in the UK.

---

1 As to the meaning of objective criteria, at least in another regime, see para 14 in *Jeen Lolkes Posthumus* v *Rinze & Anne Oosterwoud* [1992] 2 CMLR 336.
2 Article 6.6 of Council Regulation 805/68 as amended by Council Regulation 2066/92.
3 Article 4(i) of Council Regulation 805/68 as amended by Council Regulation 2066/92. See also Articles 46-52 of Commission Regulation 3886/92 for detailed rules.
4 Article 6(a)2 of Council Regulation 805/68 as amended by Council Regulation 2066/92.
5 Article 6(a)3 of Council Regulation 805/68 as amended by Council Regulation 2066/92.

Beef special premium and suckler cow premium common features of the schemes

12.1   Common definitions

The basic definitions are provided in the Council Regulation.[1] Producer is defined as an individual farmer, whether a natural or legal person or group of natural or legal persons, irrespective of the legal status conferred by national law on such a group or its members, whose holding is located within the Community territory and who is engaged in rearing bovine animals.

It plainly covers any business configuration known to UK laws.

Holding is defined as meaning all the production units managed by the producer and located in the territory of a single Member State. This can be compared with the definition of a holding for the milk quota regime.[2]

The use of the words "production units" as opposed to "land" would appear to indicate that a producer might have more than one holding for the purpose of the EC regulations if separate enterprises are maintained on separate land.

12.2   Stocking density

12.2.1   The concept

In broad terms, to be eligible to claim both beef special premium and suckler cow premium a producer must establish that his holding is not over-stocked. This could have been a far-reaching provision of the implementation package for both regimes and on the face of it is central to the Community's attempts to reward extensive and environmentally friendly methods of farming. While it will have relatively little impact at the outset, by 1995 or 1996 it is likely to have a very significant impact on the manner in which some producers organise their farming businesses and the levels of rent paid for forage area. Initially the maximum stocking density rate is set at 3.5 livestock units per hectare of forage area which many existing UK farming businesses will be able to comply with without any alteration to farm policy. However, by 1996 stocking density rates have to be reduced by 43% to 2.0 livestock units per hectare of forage area. This is likely to cause substantial change to some businesses.

On closer examination, however, the stocking density concept is, like much of the regime, lacking in integrity. No doubt partly to make administration simpler, the actual calculation of stocking density has been devised on an extremely standardised format, including only certain groups of animals – those in fact which are directly supported by the EC. The result of this is that, in practice, a highly intensive and even over-

---

1   Article 4a of Council Regulation 805/68 as amended.
2   Article 9(d) of Council Regulation 3950/92.

stocked farm could receive very substantial beef premium support and even claim the so-called "extensification premium". This will be further explained later. Although the introduction of the stocking density concept may eventually cause some farmers to change their production systems, it really amounts to little more than a device for limiting the total support per business.

12.2.2   Who is subject to stocking density?
Any producer claiming either beef special premium or suckler cow premium and who has had to submit the IACS area aid application[1] is subject to the stocking density rules to test eligibility for beef special premium and/or suckler cow premium.[2] The IACS area aid application is mandatory for any farmer claiming any of the aids covered by IACS and these are the aid schemes for arable crops, the premium scheme for sheep meat and goat meat, HLCAs and of course beef special premium and suckler cow premium.[3] Once a producer is within the IACS net and submits an application for either beef special premium or suckler cow premium the competent authority of the Member State has to establish the number of livestock units and forage area and thus arrive at stocking density.[4]

12.2.3   Small producers
The only exception is the small producer keeping so few animals that total livestock units do not exceed 15. Any producer can claim as a small producer by only claiming up to 15 livestock units. Because beef cattle for which no premium are claimed do not count as livestock units even producers rearing intensive beef with bought-in feed will be able to claim premium on a limited number of animals (a maximum of 25 head if under 24 months old).

Small producers exempt from the stocking density rules do not have to complete the IACS form unless claiming either extensification premium[5] or arable aid.[6]

12.2.4   Stocking density rules
The total number of animals qualifying for beef special premium and suckler cow premium is limited by the application of the stocking density rate on the holding.[7]

The stocking density ratios are (see table on p74):

---

1   Article 6.1 of Council Regulation 3508/92.
2   Article 42.1 of Commission Regulation 3886/92.
3   Article 1 of Council Regulation 3508/92.
4   Article 42 of Commission Regulation 3886/92.
5   Article 4(h) of Council Regulation 805/68 as amended.
6   Article 42.1 of Commission Regulation 3886/92.
7   Article 4g(1) of Council Regulation 805/68 as amended by Council Regulation 2066/92.

	Livestock units per ha of forage area	Livestock units per acre of forage area
1993	3.5	1.41
1994	3.0	1.21
1995	2.5	1.01
1996 onwards	2.0	0.81

Even if these stocking rates applied to all livestock on the holding, they are not particularly extensive. At 2.0 LU per forage hectare (0.8 LU per acre or 1.23 acres per LU), this is more extensive than many livestock farms in UK lowland conditions, but the calculation does not have to include all livestock so that forage area used by livestock outside the scope of the legislation can be included in the calculation against the animals that are included.

To determine the stocking density one has to identify the livestock units to be applied to the animals on the holding and the forage area of the holding.

12.2.4(a)   Livestock units

The livestock units are calculated by taking into account all the male bovine animals, suckler cows, sheep (or goats) for which premium applications have been submitted and in addition the notional number of dairy cows required to fill the producer's milk quota. The number of animals on a holding is converted into livestock units at the following rate

Dairy cows	1.0 LU
Breeding ewes on which Sheep Annual Premium has been claimed	0.15 LU
Male cattle on which Beef Special Premium has been claimed, aged under 2 years on the date of the claim	0.6 LU
Male cattle on which Beef Special Premium has been claimed, aged 2 years and over on the date of the claim	1.0 LU
Suckler cows on which Suckler Cow Premium has been claimed (including replacement in-calf heifers)	1.0 LU[1]

All other livestock on the holding not falling in the above categories are ignored for the purpose of calculating livestock units.

Dairy farms

However, before getting to the exercise of calculating the number of actual livestock units on the holding, allowance has to be made for the dairy cows necessary to produce the amount of milk to fill the milk

---

1   Article 4g(3) of Council Regulation 805/68 as amended and Annex I to Council Regulation 2328/91.

quota allocated to the producer.[1] It is assumed that a producer's dairy cow numbers are the number that would be required to produce the milk quota allocated to the producer based on the UK average milk yield.[2] The UK average milk yield is set at 5,200 kgs (5,050 ltrs) per cow for 1993.[3] The actual number of cows used is disregarded. This is a rough and ready rule and fails to distinguish between producers of high and low yields whether of butterfat or milk. Thus, a producer might have a high-performing herd of 100 cows giving large yields at high butterfat levels requiring a milk quota of 700,000 ltrs. A more pedestrian producer might require 140 cows to produce the same volume of milk quota. Regardless of these differences both producers will be treated as having 139 livestock units attributable to their dairy herd (700,000 ÷ 5,050 = 138.6).

Non-producing producers will be in the interesting position of having imputed dairy cows allocated to them even though they have no cows.

Another interesting feature of the regime is that it is the amount of milk quota which is registered in the producer's name on April 1 which is used to calculated livestock units. Producers have to undertake not to increase their milk quotas for a period of 12 months from the date when they make their application for suckler cow premium.[4] This may cover a period of more than one year for the purpose of leasing or transferring milk quotas since the milk quota year runs from April 1 to March 31.[5]

12.2.4(b)   Forage area

Forage area is defined[6] as the area of the holding which:

(i)   is available throughout the calendar year for rearing bovine animals and sheep or goats
(ii) does not include buildings, woods, ponds or paths
(iii) does not include land for which area aid is claimed under the arable area payment system (including set-aside land)
(iv) does not include areas used for other crops benefiting from community aid
(v)   does not include land used for permanent crops or horticultural crops[7]

The Scottish Office IACS form permits open wooded areas to which stock have access and which make a significant contribution to grazing

---

1   Article 42.3 of Commission Regulation 3886/92.
2   Article 42.3 of Commission Regulation 3886/92.
3   Article 25 and Annex III of Commission Regulation 3886/92.
4   Article 24.1(b) of Commission Regulation 3886/92.
5   Article 1 of Council Regulation 3950/92 .
6   Article 4g(3) of Council Regulation 805/68 as amended by Council Regulation 2066/92 and note the slightly different definition for IACS purposes contained in Article 2 of Commission Regulation 3887/92.
7   However set aside land under (a) of the third sub-paragraph of Article 2(3) of Council Regulation 2328/91 is not excluded (grazing for extensive livestock farming on set aside arable land – in the UK the grazed fallow option under the five year set aside scheme).

(eg orchard) needs to be counted as forage area. Grassland is counted as a full hectare whether it is at the top of a mountain or is the best river meadow.

Just because land is used for growing crops which are eligible for arable area aid does not mean that such land cannot be counted as forage area. If no claim for arable area aid payments is made then apparently the land may be counted as forage area. It is this flexibility which leads to the need for very careful consideration of the producer's forage area.

It is the area determined under the IACS procedure (whether forage or otherwise) which is taken for calculating stocking density.[1]

Shared use

The producer's forage area includes areas in shared use and areas subject to mixed cultivation.[2] The areas in shared use are accredited to the holding's forage area in proportion to the share of total grazing rights on that area.[3]

Priority of deductions

The order of priority for deducting livestock units is

(i) the necessary livestock units to accommodate the milk quota on April 1[4]

(ii) the necessary livestock units to accommodate the sheep or goats for which premium is claimed[5]

If there are any livestock units left over having deducted these two classes of livestock unit then the balance can be used to claim either beef special premium or suckler cow premium.[6]

The following example shows how the calculation might work:

Stocking density calculation

1. Eligible stock   LU

	LU
100 "imputed" dairy cows @ 1.0	100
600 Ewes @ 0.15	90
90 Beef Special Premium @ 0.6(<24m)	54
	244

2. Forage area = 100ha

3. Maximum livestock units

	ha	stocking rates		maximum LU's
1993	100	x	3.5	= 350
1994	100	x	3.0	= 300
1995	100	x	2.5	= 250
1996	100	x	2.0	= 200

---

1   Article 42.4(a) of Commission Regulation 3886/92.
2   Article 4g(3) of Council Regulation 805/68 as amended by Council Regulation 2066/92.
3   Article 2.1 of Commission Regulation 3887/92.
4   Article 42.4(b) of Commission Regulation 3886/92.
5   Article 42.4(c) of Commission Regulation 3886/92.
6   Article 42.4 of Commission Regulation 3886/92.

The example shows that, for the first three years of the regime this business would have no difficulty in claiming all 90 beef special premium. However, in 1996 the business falls short by some 44 livestock units. In this situation the whole beef special premium is not lost, but available livestock units can be used up. In the example the 10 livestock units remaining would allow 16 beef special premium to be claimed at the first age group (16 x 0.6 = 9.6 livestock units).

12.2.5   Extensification

There is an additional premium of a further 30 ECUs per premium granted if the stocking density on a producer's holding during a calendar year is less than 1.4 livestock units per hectare.[1] This means a further £28.17 per head on both special premium and suckler cow premium in 1993 and detailed calculations to investigate the merit of achieving this level of claim are likely to be justified on certain types of holding.

Unless the producer is exempt from stocking density rules it is not necessary for the producer to apply separately for the extensification premium.[2] It will be paid automatically at the same time as the final payment of beef special premium or suckler cow premium.[3] However, a producer exempt from stocking density rules who would not otherwise have to complete an IACS form must have done so by May 15 1993.

Many beef producers in the less-favoured areas with substantial areas of hill grazings will automatically qualify for the extensification premium without any changes to their stocking levels. It is also theoretically possible for an intensive barley/beef producer with no actual grassland to claim beef special premium and extensification premium by using cereal land as forage.

12.3   IACS

It is at this point that the purpose and use of the integrated administration and control system can be readily appreciated. From the information returned by UK producers in their IACS form verification of the eligibility to beef special premium and suckler cow premium according to stocking density rates will be obtained. In the IACS form each producer[4] will eventually have to supply full details of his forage area, milk quota and claims for sheep annual premium. Once the forage area required to meet the needs of the dairy and sheep enterprises (in that order) has been calculated there may be a residual forage area which will give the number of livestock units available to determine entitlement of the beef special premium and suckler cow premium.
In practice the UK authorities have indicated that if there are not enough livestock units available on the holding to permit all the claims

---

1   Article 4h(1) of Council Regulation 805/68 as amended and Article 43.1 of Commission
    Regulation 3886/92.
2   Article 43.2 of Commission Regulation 3886/92.
3   Article 43.3 of Commission Regulation 3886/92.
4   Unless exempted as a small producer - Article 4g(1) of Council Regulation 805/68 as
    amended by Council Regulation 2066/92.

made for beef special premium and suckler cow premium a reduction in the number of claims permitted will be made. Producers will be able to choose which claim they wish to abandon, but producers will be assumed to want to make the reduction which costs them least.

12.4 Animal identification

Any bovine animal for which beef special premium or suckler cow premium is claimed must be properly identified and then the identification details have to be kept in a special record by each producer.[1]

12.5 Hormonal substances

If there is any breach of the rules relating to substances having a hormonal action the animals concerned are automatically disqualified from receiving either beef special premium or suckler cow premium for their entire lives.[2]

12.6 Date of applications

The date when applications are submitted determines the year of the application for beef special premium and suckler cow premium.[3] This is important because the rate of payment per annum may be rising in the first years but against this will have to be set the reducing permitted stocking density rates.

12.7 Expenditure

The expenditure involved in granting beef special premium and suckler cow premium and any additional premium for extensification is treated as intervention measures.[4]

---

1 Article 4g(4) of Council Regulation 805/68 as amended by Council Regulation 2066/92 and "alphanumeric identification and registration of animals" in the chapter on IACS below.
2 Article 4j of Commission Regulation 805/68 as amended and Article 2 of Council Directive 88/146.
3 Article 45 of Commission Regulation 3886/92.
4 Article 4(l) and Article 3.1 of Council Regulation 729/70.

Beef special premium

13.1 Regions

For the beef special premium scheme Member States are either taken as a whole or divided into regions.[1] The UK has opted for three regions:

- England and Wales
- Scotland
- Northern Ireland

13.2 Regional ceilings

For each region a ceiling has to be set (regional ceiling), which is based upon the number of claims under the old system in a reference year. Member States can choose 1990, 1991 or 1992, but one year had to apply to each Member State and different regions could not have different reference years.[2] The UK has chosen 1991 as the reference year giving regional ceilings of approximately:

England and Wales	940,000
Scotland	244,000
Northern Ireland	234,000

Member States have the option of allocating individual ceilings to producers but the UK have not taken this route. If the total number of valid claims for animals in the 10 months to 21 months age bracket in a region exceeds that region's ceiling for one year then the number of claims per producer is reduced proportionately.[3]

Thus, if for 1993 the number of valid claims received in England and Wales turns out to be 990,000 compared with the regional ceiling of 940,000 each producer's claim will be scaled down by a factor of 5.05%. If this gives something other than a whole number then the first figure after the decimal point is taken and a corresponding fraction of a unit of premium is paid.

So if a producer claimed on the maximum of 180 animals, using the 5.05 factor above, his claim would be scaled down to 170.9 animals and the payment in 1993 would be:

170	x	56.34	=	£9,577.80
0.9	x	56.34	=	£50.70
Total				£9,628.50

---

1 Article 4b(3)(a) of Council Regulation 805/68 as amended by Council Regulation 2066/92.
2 Article 4b(3)(b) of Council Regulation 805/68 as amended by Council Regulation 2066/92.
3 Article 4b(3) of Council Regulation 805/68 as amended by Council Regulation 2066/92.

13.3   Annual premium

The premium is available annually on male cattle only.[1] Annually means by reference to a calendar year.[2]

13.4   Amount of premium

The amount of beef special premium per eligible animal is set at

1993	60 ECUs per head
1994	75 ECUs per head
1995 onwards	95 ECUs per head[3]

The green pound conversion rate applied for the purpose of calculating beef special premium is that prevailing at January 1.[4] The exchange rate on January 1 1993 was 1 ECU = £0.939052 giving a beef special premium rate of £56.34 per head. Assuming the same rate of exchange in 1994 and 1995 gives rates of £70.42 per head and £84.51 per head.

13.5   Numbers and ages of animals

Premium can be claimed by a producer on up to 90 animals in each of two categories.[5] Thus there is a maximum of 180 animals per producer per year on which premiums can be claimed. The two age brackets are from 10 months and from 22 months,[6] but applications may be made for animals which on the date of commencement of the retention period (two months) are not less than eight months nor more than 20 months for the first-age bracket and not less than 21 months old for the second bracket. Animals may qualify for the premium twice in their lifetime only.[7] To obtain the premium the producer must apply[8] and any animal for which an application is made has to be retained by the producer for a minimum period of two months from the date of lodging the application.[9] Member States may specify other start dates for the retention period and the UK has done so. Producers in the UK can specify their own start date provided that it is within two months of the application being lodged. This means that producers can group together cattle of different ages in a single retention period, but all the cattle in that group must comply with the age bracket requirements. So for the first premium the earliest start date for the retention period is the date

---

1   Article 4b(i) of Council Regulation 805/68 as amended by Council Regulation 2066/92.
2   Article 4b(1) of Council Regulation 805/68 as amended by Council Regulation 2066/92.
3   Article 4b(6) of Council Regulation 805/68 as amended.
4   Article 53 of Commission Regulation 3886/92.
5   Article 4b(1) of Council Regulation 805/68 as amended by Council Regulation 2066/92.
6   Article 4b(2) of Council Regulation 805/68 as amended by Council Regulation 2066/92.
7   Article 4b(2) of Council Regulation 805/68 as amended by Council Regulation 2066/92.
8   Article 4b(1) of Council Regulation 805/68 as amended by Council Regulation 2066/92.
9   Article 4b(2) of Council Regulation 805/68 as amended by Council Regulation 2066/92
    and Article 4 of Commission Regulation 3886/92 as amended by Article 1 of Commission
    Regulation 538/93.

when the youngest animal in the group is eight months old and the latest date is the date on which the oldest animal is still less than 21 months old. For the second premium the earliest start date for the retention period is when the youngest animal reaches the age of 21 months.

13.6   On farm administration

The beef special premium scheme is administered at farm level rather than at slaughter with effect from March 31 1993 and only the new administration is dealt with in this book.

13.7   CIDs

To be eligible for beef special premium each animal must be covered by a national administrative document[1] and be properly identified.[2] This document must accompany each animal from the date when the first premium application is made. The document has to be drawn in such a way as to ensure that one premium only is granted per animal and per age bracket.[3] In England and Wales[4] this has been done by means of the cattle identification document (CID)[5] with different colourings. If no premium has been claimed the document is written with green print on a white background. Once the first premium has been claimed the document is written in blue print on a white background. After the second payment has been claimed the document is written in red print on a white background.

Where animals likely to qualify for beef special premium are traded within the Community there is a procedure for the exporter and importer to undergo[6] to ensure no barriers to trade are erected. The Member State in which the exporter is located has to issue a standard form document to the exporter[7] and on arrival in the Member State of the importer, that standard form will secure the issue of a national administrative document, if different from the standard form.[8]

13.8   Livestock aid applications

In addition to the IACS requirements[9] each livestock aid application for beef special premium has to contain:

---

1   Article 4b(7) of Council Regulation 805/68.
2   Article 7.1 of Commission Regulation 3886/92.
3   Article 3 of Commission Regulation 3886/92.
4   In Scotland it is a cattle control document (CCD) on white, then blue, then pink card.
5   Implementing the first option contained in Article 3.2 of Commission Regulation 3886/92.
6   Article 3.3 of Commission Regulation 3886/92.
7   Annex I of Commission Regulation 3886/92.
8   Article 3.3 of Commission Regulation 3886/92.
9   Article 5.1 of Commission Regulation 3887/92.

(a) a breakdown of the number of animals by age bracket and
(b) the reference to the administrative document accompanying the animal[1]

Member States can impose a minimum size of claim for each application provided that the number is not greater than three.[2] The UK has chosen not to impose any minimum size.

Member States can also choose the periods and dates for submission of applications for beef special premium and the number of applications per calendar year.[3] Originally the UK Government was proposing to limit applications for first payment of beef special premium to three times per calendar year, but due to pressure from producers and auctioneers this restriction has not been imposed and there is no limit on the number of applications that may be made in 1993.

13.9   Payments

Payments have to be made as soon as inspections have been carried out or by June 30 of the following calendar year at the latest.[4] In the UK an advance of 60% of the premium will be paid after November 1 of the year of the claim[5] with the balance after April 1 (and before June 30) in the following year ("the definitive payment").[6]

Once an application for one age bracket of beef special premium has been made in respect of an animal it is deemed to have received the premium and therefore cannot be claimed for it in any other calendar year even if no premium was in fact paid due to the application of the proportional reduction in payment caused by exceeding the regional ceiling or the application of the density factor on that particular producer's holding.[7]

The Beef Special Premium (Protection of Payments) Order 1989[8] and the Beef Special Premium (Recovery Powers) Regulations 1989[9] are due to be revoked and replaced.

13.10   Deseasonalisation premium

In addition to the beef special premium there is available a deseasonalisation premium of 60 ECUs per male castrated animal[10] which has already benefited from the beef special premium and which is slaughtered between January 1 and April 30 of the following year.

---

1 Article 2 of Commission Regulation 3886/92.
2 Article 41.1 of Commission Regulation 3886/92.
3 Article 41.2 of Commission Regulation 3886/92.
4 Article 4b(6) Council Regulation 805/68 as amended.
5 Article 44.1 of Commission Regulation 3886/92.
6 Article 44.2 of Commission Regulation 3886/92.
7 Article 7.2 of Commission Regulation 3886/92.
8 1989 SI No. 574.
9 1989 SI No. 575.
10 Article 1 of Council Regulation 125/93 amending Article 4c of Council Regulation 805/68 as amended.

For producers in a Member State to be eligible the number of male castrated animals in the Member State to be slaughtered between September 1 and November 30 has to exceed 40% of the total number of castrated male cattle slaughtered in that year.[1]

The UK obtained specific dispensation to have Northern Ireland treated as a separate entity with the result that the deseasonalisation premium will apply in Northern Ireland while not currently being available in the remaining regions of the UK.[2]

In Northern Ireland the premium is to be paid to the producer who last held the animal prior to slaughter[3] and this may not be the recipient of beef special premium. Applications have to be submitted to the competent authority and be accompanied by a slaughterhouse certificate showing:

(a) the name and address of the slaughterhouse where slaughter took place
(b) the identity and slaughter number of the animal
(c) the date of slaughter[4]

In Northern Ireland the Beef Special Premium (Protection of Payments) Regulations (N Ireland) 1989[5] are due to be revoked and replaced.

13.11 Administration

In England and Wales the beef special premium scheme is administered by MAFF's regional service centres, not the Intervention Board and in Scotland through local area offices of SOAFD.

---

1 Article 4c(1) of Council Regulation 805/68 as amended by Council Regulation 2066/92.
2 Article 4c(1) of Council Regulation 805/68 as amended.
3 Article 20 of Commission Regulation 3886/92.
4 Article 21 of Commission Regulation 3886/92.
5 1989 SI No. 127

Suckler cow premium

14.1 Definitions

The definitions of producer and holding have already been referred to. The definition of a suckler cow is:

(i) a cow belonging to a meat breed or born of a cross with a meat breed, and belonging to a herd intended for rearing calves for meat production; and
(ii) an in-calf heifer, meeting the same criteria, which replaces a suckler cow[1]

The bovine breeds which are not treated as meat breeds are:

"Angler Rotvieh (Angeln) – Rod dansk maeikerace (RMD),
Ayrshire
Armoricaine
Bretonne Pie-noire
Fries-Hollands (FH), Francaise frisonne pie noire (FFPN), Friesian-Holstein, Holstein Black and White Friesian, Red and White Friesian, Frisona espoñala. Frisona Italiana. Zwarbonten van België/Pie nire de Belgique. Sortbroget dansk mæikerace (SDM), Deutsche Schwarzbunte. Schwarzbunte Milchrasse (SMR).
Groninger Blaarkop
Guernsey
Jersey
Kerry
Malkeborthorn
Reggiana
Valdostana Nera.[2]

As a transitional measure, although cows of dairy breeds are no longer eligible even if put to a beef bull, for 1993 and 1994 there is an exception to allow premium to be claimed if it can be proved that:

• the cow was put to a beef bull
• the farmer claimed a suckler cow premium on dairy cows covered with a beef bull in 1990 or 1991
• the number of dairy cows does not exceed the number on which premium was received in 1990 or 1991 or the farmer's suckler cow quota limit.[3]

This transitional measure was introduced following pressure from Ireland where a high proportion of the suckler cow herd has been old dairy cows.

---

1 Article 4a of Council Regulation 805/68 as amended by Council Regulation 2066/92.
2 Article 22 and Annex II of Commission Regulation 3886/92.
3 Article 58 of Commission Regulation 3886/92.

Whether cows belong to a suckler herd or to a dairy herd has to be checked on the basis of the producer's milk quota and an average milk yield.[1] The average milk yield is either the one specified in Annex III of 3886/92 which for the UK is 5,050 ltrs per cow or a Member State can allow a producer to prove his dairy herd's average yield by reference to appropriate documentation.[2]

14.2 Eligibility for premium

The suckler cow premium is payable to producers of breeding cows belonging to a herd used for the production of calves for beef rearing.[3] Unlike beef special premium there is no 90 cow limit to the number of premium that can be claimed per producer. The major change in the rules for the scheme is the introduction of individual quotas for premium rights at producer level.[4]

14.2.1 Dairy farms
To be eligible for the suckler cow premium the producer must not supply milk or milk products from his farm for 12 months from the day when he lodges his application.[5] Milk and milk products are defined in the milk quota regime as "the produce of the milking of one or more cow" and "cream butter and cheese in particular".[6]

However, there is an exemption for dairy farmers making direct sales who are entitled to claim suckler cow premium without restriction.[7] The definition of direct sales is the supply of milk or milk products directly from the holding to the consumer which, not surprisingly, is the same definition as is adopted for the purposes of the milk quota regime.[8] In addition there is an exemption for small dairy farmers whose milk quota does not exceed 120,000 kgs (116,538 ltrs) provided they comply with the retention period.[9]

14.2.2 Retention period
The grant of premium is conditional upon the producer complying with a retention period of six months immediately following the day the application for suckler cow premium is lodged.[10] The requirement is to maintain a number of suckler cows at least equal to the number for which the premium was requested.[11]

---

1 Article 4d(6) and Annex III of 3886/92.
2 Article 25 of Commission Regulation 3886/92.
3 Article 4d(1) of Council Regulation 805/68 as amended by Council Regulation 2066/92.
4 Article 4d(2) of Council Regulation 805/68 as amended by Council Regulation 2066/92 and Article 27.1 of Commission Regulation 3886/92.
5 Article 4d(5) of Council Regulation 805/68 as amended.
6 Article 9(a) and (b) of Council Regulation 3950/92.
7 Article 4d(5) of Council Regulation 805/68 as amended.
8 Article 9(h) of Council Regulation 3950/92.
9 Article 4d(6) of Council Regulation 805/68 as amended.
10 Article 23 of Commission Regulation 3886/92.
11 Article 4d(5) of Council Regulation 805/68 as amended by Council Regulation 2066/92.

14.3   Allocation of quota

Suckler cow premium quotas are allocated according to the number of animals for which a premium was granted in respect of the reference year.[1] The number claimed in the reference year is the starting point but a deduction for the setting up of a national reserve is imposed. Member States were free to choose 1990, 1991 or 1992 as their reference year. The UK chose 1992 as its reference year because it was likely to maximise the overall availability of quota.

For producers who did not receive premium payments in the reference year or received a lesser number than they otherwise would due to natural circumstances there is flexibility to choose the number of payments made in the closest reference year.[2] In the UK this will mean going back to 1991

14.3.1   Natural circumstances
Natural circumstances are defined for these purposes[3] as being any of the following events provided that they happened before the application date or closing date for applications in the reference year (1992 in the UK):

- there was a reduction in the number of animals ascribed to natural circumstances affecting the herd provided that the competent authority is informed within 10 days of the producer becoming aware of the incident
- a serious natural disaster having a major effect on the producer's holding
- accidental destruction of the producer's forage resources or buildings intended for rearing his suckler cow herd
- an epizootic which led to the slaughter of at least half of the producer's suckler cow herd.

The number of claims made in the reference year is based on the number of valid claims for which payment was made and if penalties were incurred then the reduced number resulting from those penalties is applied.[4]

Producers have to be told their suckler cow premium quota by October 31 1993 (including any additional rights)[5] but if there is a dispute as to the amount of his quota the award may be provisional.[6]

---

1 Article 27.2 of Commission Regulation 3886/92.
2 Article 4d(3) of Council Regulation 805/68 as amended and Article 28(a) of Commission Regulation 3886/92.
3 Article 28(b) of Commission Regulation 3886/92 and compare the more restrictive definition of natural circumstances in the sheep regime entitling a producer to an alternative reference year to 1991.
4 Article 4d(3) of Council Regulation 805/68 and Article 27.4 of Commission Regulation 3886/92.
5 Article 27.3 of Commission Regulation 3886/92 as amended by Article 1 of Commission Regulation 583/93.
6 Article 27.3 of Commission Regulation 3886/92.

14.3.2   Additional rights

The Council have created additional rights to suckler cow premium quota which are added to the national reserves of Member States. These are to be allocated from national reserves in the first instance to milk producers who for the first time are eligible to claim suckler cow premium due to the increase in size of the exemption for small dairy farmers from 60,000 kgs[1] to 120,000 kgs.[2]

Applications for additional rights have to be made in a period to be specified by the Member State between February 15 and May 15.[3] The UK has laid down a period up to May 15 1993[4]. Applications for additional rights have to specify:[5]

- the name and address of the producer
- the number of additional premium rights applied for
- a declaration by the producer that from January 1 1993 he has kept a number of eligible suckler cows equal to the number of additional rights applied for and premium rights already acquired
- an undertaking by the producer to keep the number of cows referred to until June 30 1993
- a declaration stating the producer's milk quota on April 1 1993.

Applications for additional rights are subject to the same provisions of IACS[6] and the same penalties for misdeclaration apply.[7]

The UK has been awarded 118,320 additional rights to suckler cow premium.[8] Recipients of additional quota have to have kept their suckler cows on their holding continuously between January 1 1993 and June 30 1993.

Producers who did qualify for suckler cow premium because their milk quotas were less than 60,000 kgs are also eligible for additional rights. These producers were limited to 10 claims for suckler cow premium[9] and now they can claim for the full number of suckler cows actually kept. However, they cannot benefit twice over from ordinary suckler cow premium rights and additional suckler cow premium rights and any ordinary premium rights obtained are taken into account when awarding additional rights.[10]

The deduction to create the national reserve is applied equally to beneficiaries of additional premium rights.[11]

Any unallocated additional rights are added to the national reserve and distributed in the normal way. If there is a shortfall of additional

---

1 Article 2(a) of Council Regulation 1357/80 as amended by Council Regulation 1187/90.
2 Article 4d(6) of Council Regulation 805/68 as amended by Council Regulation 2066/92.
3 Article 30a.1 of Commission Regulation 3886/92 as amended by Commission Regulation 583/93.
4 MAFF Form SCP13 and Guidance Notes SCP14.
5 Article 30a.1 of Council Regulation 3886/92 as amended by 538/93.
6 Commission Regulation 3887/92.
7 Article 10 of Commission Regulation 3887/92.
8 Annex II of Council Regulation 125/93.
9 Article 2(c) of Council Regulation 1357/80 as amended by Council Regulation 1187/90.
10 Article 4d(6) of Council Regulation 805/68 as amended by Council Regulation 2066/92.
11 Article 4d(6) of Council Regulation 805/86 as amended by Council Regulation 2066/92.

rights scaling down is applied although certain priority categories of claimant may be favoured.[1]

14.3.3   Extensification programmes

A producer who has complied with a Community extensification programme scheme[2] can apply for extra premium rights when his scheme expires.[3] His extra allocation is the difference between the number of claims for suckler cow premium in the year when he commenced his scheme and the number of premium rights claimed in 1992. These additional rights cannot be leased or transferred for three years[4] and if the producer does not use all of his rights during the three-year period the average number of rights not used over that period is withdrawn from him and put into the national reserve.

14.3.4   National reserves

Every Member State is obliged to set up a national reserve equal to at least 1% but nor more than 3% of the total number of animals for which suckler cow premium is granted in the reference year. To this can be added any premium rights going to the national reserve via the syphon.[5]

The UK is likely to base it's initial national reserve on 1% of the premiums allocated in 1992 giving a reserve of approximately 16,000 suckler cow premium rights. The UK Government apparently considered that there was likely to be a substantial surplus of additional rights[6] which could be added to the national reserve.

Member States are given a relatively wide range of producers to whom they can award suckler cow premium rights from the national reserve. These are:

(a) producers who applied for a premium before January 1 1993 and who prove that the application of suckler cow premium quotas would put at risk the viability of their holdings taking account of the implementation of an investment programme in beef drawn up before January 1 1993

(b) producers who have submitted in respect of the reference year a premium application which as a result of exceptional circumstances does not correspond to the actual situation as established during the previous years

(c) producers who have regularly submitted premium applications without, however, having submitted an application in reference year

(d) producers who submit a premium application for the first time during the year following the reference year or in subsequent years

(e) producers who have acquired part of the land previously used for cattle breeding by other producers.

---

1   Article 4d(6) of Council Regulation 805/68 as amended by Council Regulation 2066/92.
2   Council Regulation 797/85.
3   Article 38.3 of Commission Regulation 3886/92.
4   Article 38.3(a) of Commission Regulation 3886/92.
5   Article 4f(1) of Council Regulation 805/68 as amended by Council Regulation 2066/92.
6   Article 4d(6) of Council Regulation 805/68 as amended by Council Regulation 2066/92.

After a limited consultation period (June 25 1992 to February 15 1993) the categories and priority of producers able to claim from the national reserve are to be set out in a statutory instrument, which will also have to set up a suitable machinery for dealing with claims.

The community legislation[1] also required an additional reserve to be created consisting of 1% of the total quota of producers in less favoured areas of each Member State. This additional reserve is for the exclusive use of producers in less favoured areas according to criteria laid down by Member States.

14.3.5   Rights from the national reserve
A producer receiving suckler cow premium free of charge from the national reserve cannot sell these rights or lease them for the following three calendar years.[2] Furthermore if he does not fully utilise all the premium rights the average of the rights not used over the three years is withdrawn from the producer and returned to the national reserve.[3]

14.3.6   Utilisation of rights (not from the national reserve)
Quite apart from the sanction for non utilisation against producers receiving premium rights from the national reserve, if a producer fails to utilise at least half of his rights during two consecutive calendar years the amount of rights that he fails to use in the second year are taken from him and put into the national reserve.[4] There is an exception for exceptional circumstances cases. These are not defined but presumably would include force majeure and might go further than that and might include "natural circumstances"[5] as well as anything else that was truly exceptional.

14.4   Transfers and leases of quota

14.4.1   Transfers of rights with land
Producers may transfer or lease their suckler cow premium rights in certain circumstances. If a producer sells or otherwise transfers his holding he has the option of transferring all his suckler cow premium rights to the person taking over his holding without deduction to the national reserve.[6] This person may or may not himself be a producer. A sale is specified as a potential occasion of transfer but the question is what other occasions amount to transfers. Fuller words are utilised in the milk quota regime,[7] and cases under that regime are likely to provide some assistance. Thus, inheritance either on death or during lifetime is likely to qualify for transfer without deduction to the national

---

1   Article 4f(3) of Council Regulation 805/68 as amended and Article 31 of Commission Regulation 3886/92.
2   Article 32(a) of Commission Regulation 3886/92.
3   Article 32(b) of Commission Regulation 3886/92.
4   Article 33 of Commission Regulation 3886/92.
5   See Article 28 of Commission Regulation 3886/92.
6   Article 4e.1 of Council Regulation 805/68 as amended by Commission Regulation 2066/92.
7   Article 7 of Council Regulation 3950/92 and its predecessor Council Regulation 857/84.

reserve.[1] Equally the dissolution of the partnership with accompanying changes in occupation of the holding, albeit without changes in the land ownership rights, may qualify.[2]

14.4.2   Transfers without land
Where a producer transfers all or part of his suckler cow premium rights to other producers without transferring his holding there is a syphon to the national reserve.[3] The maximum level at which the syphon can be set is 15%. The premium rights syphoned to the national reserve are removed without compensation and from the national reserve they are redistributed free of charge to newcomers or priority producers.[4]

14.4.3   Transfers of part
If a producer wishes to transfer a part of his premium rights without the transfer of his holding the minimum number that he can transfer is five if he has more than 25 premium rights or three if he has between 10 and 25 premium rights. If he has less than 10 premium rights Member States can specify the minimum number of rights that can be transferred. This cannot exceed three and Member States have to take the decision "on the basis of their production structures". Presumably this means that for the UK a higher rather than a lower figure would be justified but for some Mediterranean Member States where small producers are more common a lower figure would be justified.[5]

14.4.4   Leasing
Premium rights have to be leased for a whole calendar year and the same minimum number of rights per lease apply as when transferring part of producers premium rights. However, there is a limit on the frequency and volume of leasing that a producer may undertake. Over a five-year period starting from when he first leases quota a producer has to use all of his premium rights himself in two consecutive calendar years. If he fails to do this his quota becomes unleasable. There is an exception for producers participating in the community extensification programme if the Member State concerned makes provision to extend the five-year period according to the duration of the extensification programme.[6]

14.4.5   Formalities on transfers and leasing
The transfer or a lease is only effective after both parties to the agreement have notified the competent authorities in the Member State. Accordingly, it is going to be important for purchasers and lessees to have obtained an irrevocable form of notification before parting company

---

1   *Siegfried Rauh v Hauptzollant Nurnberg-Furth* (Case C 314/89) OJ/91/C105 p12.
2   *Faulks v Faulks* [1992] 15 EG 82.
3   Article 4e.1 of Council Regulation 805/68 as amended by Council Regulation 2066/92.
4   Article 4f(2) of Council Regulation 805/68 as amended by Council Regulation 2066/92.
5   Article 34.1 of Council Regulation 3886/92.
6   Article 34.3 of Commission Regulation 3886/92.

with money.[1]

There will be time-limits for notifying the competent authorities for transfer or lease. The 1993 notification date can be fixed by Member States in their discretion because of the difficulties involved in the start up of the system, but in subsequent years while Member States retain a certain amount of discretion they must specify a date which allows at least two months for applications to be submitted.[2]

Where a transfer or lease is effected producers have to be notified of their new quotas.[3]

14.4.6   Transfers by commons graziers

A producer who only farms on land in which he has no property right because it is publicly owned or collectively owned and who decides to stop farming this land and to transfer all his rights to another producer is not liable to any deductions to the national reserve. The only form of grazing right which is publicly or collectively owned in the UK is commons grazing. But even the commons grazier, if he does not meet all these conditions, is subject to deductions to the national reserve.[4] Nothing less than stopping farming (presumably this means on a permanent basis) and disposing of all his quota to another producer will avoid the national reserve.

14.4.7   Partial rights

When carrying out any calculations relating to suckler cow premium only the first number after the document print is taken into account.[5] All of the partial rights held by a producer or to be transferred to the national reserve have to be added together.[6] Partial rights carry partial entitlement to premium according to the fraction of the unit amount of the premium.[7]

14.4.8   Ring fences

Member States are obliged to take the necessary precautions to avoid suckler cow premium rights being moved away from sensitive zones or regions where beef production is especially important for the local economy.[8] The UK Government has accordingly proposed the following "ring fences"

(i)   the lowlands in Great Britain
(ii)   the English less favoured areas
(iii)   the Welsh less favoured areas
(iv)   the Scottish less favoured areas

---

1   Article 34.2 of Commission Regulation 3886/92.
2   Second paragraph of article 34.2 of Commission Regulation 3886/92.
3   Article 35 of Commission Regulation 3886/92.
4   Article 36 Commission Regulation 3886/92.
5   Article 40.1 of Commission Regulation 3886/92.
6   Article 40.2 of Commission Regulation 3886/92.
7   Article 40.3 of Commission Regulation 3886/92.
8   Article 4e(2) of Council Regulation 805/68 as amended by Council Regulation 2066/92.

(v)   the Northern Irish less favoured areas

(vi) the Northern Irish lowlands

(viii)the Scottish highlands and islands.

It is proposed that ring fences will apply not only to quota movements but also to producers, so that if a farmer moves out of a "ring fence" it would not normally be possible for his quota to move with him. The only exception would be where the producer's holding lies in both LFA and non-LFA land. If such a producer acquired or disposed of land then he would be able to change his quota designation so as to reflect the new situation.

Member States have the option of causing all transfers of premium rights unaccompanied by transfers of holdings to be carried out via the national reserve, but the UK has not chosen to adopt this route, preferring rather to leave producers to deal directly with each other.[1]

14.4.9   Landlord and tenant problems

The Council Regulation enabling transfers and leases of suckler cow premium rights recognised that Member States might encounter problems where producers who were not owners of their holdings transferred or leased their rights. In the Commission Regulation Member States are directed to adopt "appropriate transitional measures" so as to find "fair solutions" to the landlord and tenant problems that may arise when premium rights are transferred by the tenant. This is a tantalising provision which at least recognises that problems may occur and that fair solutions may be necessary.[2] The fair solution has to be based on the concept of suckler cow premium being a producer-linked premium right[3] in contrast to milk quota which is a land-linked form of quota.[4] The conceptual difficulty lies in ascertaining the type of problem that can occur in a property right transaction, such as a lease, when considering a right that is said not to be linked to land.

The UK Government will not have been greatly assisted in its search for fair solutions by the inability of various interested bodies to even agree on the nature of the problem. The complexities of the issues raised can be judged from the fact that there are respected organisations and eminent chartered surveyors all with strongly differing views.

14.5   Applications for suckler cow premium

Over and above the IACS requirements for livestock aid applications[5] any application for suckler cow premium has to contain:

(i) the producer's milk quota at April 1 in the calendar year concerned[6]

---

1   Article 4e.2(b) of Council Regulation 805/68 as amended by Council Regulation 2066/92.
2   Article 39 of Commission Regulation 3886/92.
3   Article 39 of Commission Regulation 3886/92.
4   Council Regulation 3950/92.
5   Article 5.1 of Commission Regulation 3887/92.
6   Article 24.1(a) of Commission Regulation 3886/92.

(ii) an undertaking by the producer not to increase his milk quota for 12 months starting on the date of submission of the application.[1]

This may be a very significant undertaking which will need to be carefully considered since it may involve a producer in limiting milk production in more than one milk year. What is not clear is whether a producer may risk increasing milk production beyond his milk quota and bear the risk of paying the additional levy. From the wording of the Regulation it is possible that this would be permitted and since there is no objection to producing in excess of the milk quota and taking the risk of having to pay the additional levy there would appear to be no objection in principle.

Applications for suckler cow premium may be restricted to an overall period of six months of a calendar year in the discretion of Member States.[2]

As with the special premium applications, Member States can impose a minimum size of claim for each application provided the number is not greater than three.[3] The UK has chosen not to impose any minimum size.

Member States can chose the periods and dates for submissions of suckler cow premium applications and the number of applications per calendar year.[4] The UK normally has a limited period for submission of suckler cow premiums and the period is six months. In 1992 there was an alteration to the application period which has caused a great deal of trouble. It is likely that the application period will be six months again in 1993.

Once the IACS requirements of administrative checks and on-the-spot checks have been carried out the competent authority has to pay an advance equal to 60% of the suckler cow premium, but it cannot pay before November 1 in the year for which premium is claimed.[5]

The final payment of suckler cow premium is called the definitive payment and naturally this is the difference between the advance and the final entitlement to premium.

14.6 Payment

The amount of the suckler cow premium is set at

1993	70 ECUs
1994	95 ECUs
1995 onwards	120 ECUs[6]

---

1 Article 24.1(b) of Commission Regulation 3386/92.
2 Article 24.2 of Commission Regulation 3386/92.
3 Article 41.1 of Commission Regulation 3386/92.
4 Article 41.2 of Commission Regulation 3386/92.
5 Article 44.1 of Commission Regulation 3386/92.
6 Article 4d(7) of Council Regulation 805/68 as amended by Council Regulation 2066/92.

The rate of premium in sterling is calculated according to the exchange rate at January 1[1] which for 1993 was 1 ECU = £0.939052. This means that for 1993 the rate of payment is £65.73 per head and, if the exchange rate were to remain unchanged the figure would increase to £89.20 per head for 1994 and rise to £112.68 per head from 1995 onwards. These payments compare with the 1992 rate of £55.38 and £59.64 in the LFAs.

There is provision for Member States to grant additional national premiums of up to 25 ECUs per head[2] and in LFAs the first 20 ECUs of such a premium would be financed by the guidance section of the European Agricultural Guidance and Guarantee Fund (EAGGF).[3] The UK has not chosen to grant this additional premium.

The suckler cow premium has to be paid as soon as inspections are carried out and by no later than June 30 in the calendar year following the claim. As with beef special premium, the UK proposes to make an advance on payment of 60% after November 1 in the year of claim, which it is authorised to do,[4] with final payments after April 1 (and before June 30) in the following year ("the definitive payment").[5]

---

1   Article 53 of Commission Regulation 3886/92.
2   See also Article 26 of Commission Regulation 3886/92.
3   Article 4d(7) of Council Regulation 805/68 as amended by Council Regulation 2066/92.
4   Article 44.1 of Commission Regulation 3886/92.
5   Article 44.2 of Commission Regulation 3886/92.

Beef premiums on the arable farm

15   An arable farmer, short of the necessary forage hectares in order to qualify for beef premiums under the new stocking density requirements, has a number of options:

1. Do nothing and accept a lower number of payments.
2. Rent additional forage area.
3. Use some of his cereal hectares as forage (in other words, just not claim under the cereals scheme and this has the advantage of reducing the set-aside area required).
4. Consider whether cereal hectares should be used to claim extensification premium.

In order to work out the best option a number of complex calculations have to be done and assumptions have to be made as to the eventual levels of premium or arable payments. The following examples show the complexity of the interaction between the arable and beef regimes and give some broad indications of what the alternatives may be.

Option 1
If stocking density is over the limit (3.5 livestock units per hectare in 1993) the producer does not lose all premium. Payment is made on the number of animals up to the 3.5 livestock units per hectare limit. A producer with under 15 livestock units (ie 15 suckler cows or 25 beef special premium under 24 months) does not have to pass the stocking density requirements. This means an intensive producer with no forage area can still claim up to 15 livestock units worth of premiums.

Option 2
The amount of rent that can be afforded depends on the type of animal. The tables in the appendix set out the per hectare returns for the three types of animal and show the change between 1993 and 1996. The table below summarises the payments per hectare over the 1993 to 1996 period for each class of beef animal, assuming the green pound rate at January 1 1993 and assuming no breach of the regional reference herds for beef special premium.

Summary of maximum payments per forage hectare

	Suckler cows		Beef special premium (+24m)		Beef special premium (6-24m)	
	£/ha	£/acre	£/ha	£/acre	£/ha	£/acre
1993	230	93	197	80	328	133
1994	267	108	211	85	352	142
1995	281	113	211	85	351	142
1996	225	91	169	68	281	113

It will be seen that in 1993 beef cows generate a return of £230 per ha (£93 per acre) and grass rent paid up to this level would leave the producer no better off. The extra acres may, of course, reduce fertiliser costs on the existing acres or allow additional livestock to be grazed (perhaps heifers not subject to premium or stocking density). With beef special premium the payment per hectare is very much higher for the younger age claim than for the older age claim; for the younger age claim, £328 per ha (£133 per acre) against £197 per ha (£80 per acre) for the older age claim.

Over the years the stocking density reduces, down to two livestock units by 1996, but the payments per head increase from 1993 to 1995. It will be seen from the summary table that the effect in 1994 and 1995 is to increase the grass rent "break even" point for all classes of livestock but then the "break even" rent falls back in 1996. Whether adjustments will be made to the headage payments in 1996 remains to be seen. In interpreting the summary table the following points must be borne in mind:

- all headage payments are subject to green rates applying at January 1 each year
- the suckler cow payments are relatively certain (ie not subject to the regional reference amount)
- the beef special premium payments depend on the regional reference numbers. If total claims at the first age group are in excess of the regional reference herd, the individual numbers claimed at both age groups will be scaled down proportionately. There are three different regions, England and Wales, Scotland and Northern Ireland
- both suckler cow premium and beef special premium are subject to 60% payment in November as an advance, and the balance the following year, between April and June
- rented grass can be counted as forage area so long as it is available for grazing for seven months, starting in the period January 1 to March 31, and is actually used by the claimant for at least four months of the year, and must be occupied by the claimant at May 15.

Option 3
Rather than enter the market for rented grazing, it may be worth looking at the possibility of claiming cereal land as forage rather than cereals. The comparative returns are set out in the appendix and summarised in the table at the top of p 97.

At present we do not know what the operative green pound rate will be for cereals in 1993, as this is July 1 each year. The rates used in the tables are all January 1 rates and at present the green pound rate has strengthened by approximately 5% since then. However, the tables show very clearly that whichever cereal region a beef farmer is in there could be a clear advantage from claiming cereals as forage in the early years of the scheme. However, there is a marked difference between the types of animal, with the younger age beef special premium showing an apparent advantage right up to 1996, especially if farming in Scotland LFA, Wales or Northern Ireland.

However, for the older age beef special premium there is only likely to be a clear advantage in 1993 although, depending on green rates and beef reference herds, there could be a minor advantage up to 1994. For

Comparison of forage and cereal payments per hectare

	1993 £	1994 £	1995 £	1996 £
Livestock				
Suckler cows	230	267	281	225
Beef special premium (+24m)	197	211	211	169
Beef special Premium (6-24m)	328	352	351	281
Cereals				
England	139	194	250	250
Scotland				
– Non LFA	132	185	238	238
– LFA	112	158	203	203
Wales	109	152	196	196
N Ireland	110	154	199	199

Note: 1 ECU = £0.939052

suckler cows, there looks like being an advantage in claiming cereals as forage right up to 1996 in Scotland, Wales and Northern Ireland, but quite possible no advantage by 1996 if farming in England.

For any given situation there is a large number of variables that have to be taken into account and it is essential that individual producers do their own sums for their own situation. There are a further two points that must be borne in mind:

- cereal area payments can be reduced if the regional reference area is exceeded (there are four cereal regions – England, Scotland, Wales and Northern Ireland)
- if cereal land is used as forage rather than claimed as cereals, there is a reduction in the set-aside area required and, in this situation, additional crops can be grown to generate further gross margin less extra fixed costs.

Option 4

The stocking density limit at 3.5 livestock units per forage hectare is relatively generous in 1993 and there may be few farmers finding themselves short of forage area. Some may find themselves better off claiming the extensification premium, an extra 30 ECUs (£28.17/head) by using cereals as forage. The qualification for extensification is a stocking rate of 1.4 livestock units per forage hectare and the additional payment is received on every cow or beef special premium successfully claimed. Payment is made with the final payment in April to June the following year.

Whether it is worthwhile claiming cereals as forage depends on where the starting point for stocking density is and on the opportunity to use the set-aside land released by not claiming as. Cereals Appendix II contains example calculations.

Appendix 1

Tables showing calculation of maximum payment per forage hectare for different types of beef animals compared to cereal payments

Suckler cow premium

	1993	1994	1995	1996
Livestock units	1.0	1.0	1.0	1.0
Stocking density LU/ha	3.5	3.0	2.5	2.0
Cows/ha	3.5	3.0	2.5	2.0
Payment £/head	65.7	89.2	112.6	112.6
Payment £/ha	230	267	281	225

Beef special premium (+24m)

	1993	1994	1995	1996
Livestock units	1.0	1.0	1.0	1.0
Stocking density LU/ha	3.5	3.0	2.5	2.0
No beef animals/ha	3.5	3.0	2.5	2.0
Payment £/head	56.3	70.4	84.5	84.5
Payment £/ha	197	211	211	169

Beef special premium (<24m)

	1993	1994	1995	1996
Livestock units	0.6	0.6	0.6	0.6
Stocking density LU/ha	3.5	3.0	2.5	2.0
No animals/ha	5.83	5.0	4.16	3.33
Payment £/head	56.3	70.4	84.5	84.5
Payment £/ha	328	352	351	281

Cereal payments £/ha

	1993	1994	1995	1996
England	139	194	250	250
Scotland				
– Non LFA	132	185	238	238
– LFA	112	158	203	203
Wales	109	152	196	196
N Ireland	110	154	199	199

Note 1: Beef payments determined by green rate at January 1 each year
Cereal payments determined by green rate at July 1 each year
Note 2: 1 ECU = £0.939052 (as of January 1 1993)

Appendix II

Example   100 ha cereals
                                 20 ha grass
                                 80 beef special premium claims at first age

Present stocking density
80 x 0.6   =   48 livestock units
48 LUs ÷ 20 ha =   2.4 livestock units/forage ha

Therefore well within the 1993 limit of 3.5 livestock units

Partial budget to show effect of claiming the extensification premium using the cereal area as forage

The extensification premium is £28.17/head if stocking densities are below 1.4 livestock units per ha.

This farm has 48 livestock units and so would require (48 ÷ 1.4) = 34.3 forage ha. It already has 20 ha of grass so would require an extra 14.3 ha to be claimed as forage rather than cereals. The calculation is complicated by the need to take set-aside into account.

$$14.3ha - (15\% \text{ of } 14.3ha = 2.145) = 12.155ha$$

Income foregone
12.155ha x £139 cereals payment	=	£1,689
Set-aside of 2.145ha x £250 set-aside payment	=	£ 536
		£2,225

Additional income
80 cattle at £28.17	=	£2,253
Gross margin of 2.145ha of cereals grown out of the arable scheme at £550/ha	=	£1,180
		£3,433

Additional income in this calculation is over £1,200 more by claiming cereals as forage in order to claim the extensification premium. However, it must be taken into account that:

(i)   the gross margins of crops can vary widely: also extra fixed costs must be taken into account
(ii) there will be a delay in the payment of the extensification premium
(iii) the exact arable area payments are not known. This calculations has used rates as of January 1 1993, but the actual rate will be July 1 1993.

Impact on beef farming

16   The new beef regime

It is difficult to generalise about the likely impact of the reformed beef regime on the various beef enterprises in UK agriculture. This is because there are so many variations of beef production systems and on very different scales. Furthermore, one of the major factors, that of market price, is particularly difficult to forecast. Beef prices have always been fairly volatile, depending very much on demand/supply. This can have a varying effect, depending on whether the beef farmer is a breeder, or a feeder who both buys and sells cattle. A number of comments are made below:

• Rearers of cattle, particularly suckler calf producers could be expected to benefit from these reforms as they will, for the first time, be able to claim the beef special premium on the male calves. In addition, the increased level of sucker cow premiums look attractive and, of course, existing producers are likely to have been gifted a substantial capital gain in the asset value of suckler cow quotas. In addition, if lower grain prices materialise, there will be a benefit, albeit relatively small for this grass-based enterprise, on feeding costs. Whether all this results in increased profitability for suckler calf producers, especially those in the uplands who can also relatively easily gain the extensification premium, will depend very much on how the market price for beef moves. In times of surplus production, it is very often the rearer who suffers the hardest. However, the short-term prospects look extremely good with a very strong demand for quality beef. With good marketing of a product with a "healthy" image, suckler calf producers are relatively satisfied with the reforms.

• A gross margin comparison of a lowland suckler enterprise pre and post CAP reform is set out below by way of illustration. The major assumptions are that calf sale price falls by 15% and that concentrate feed costs fall by 20%.

Suckler cow gross margin comparison
pre (1992) and post (1995) reform
1 ECU = £0.939052

	1992 £	1995 £
Output		
Calf	340	289
Beef special premium	-	42
Suckler cow premium	55	113
(Replacement cost)	(57)	(57)
Total	338	387
Variable costs		
Forage	62	62
Concentrates	49	39
Miscellaneous	43	43
Total	154	144
Gross margin per cow	184	243

The comparison shows that the price adjustments are more than compensated by the additional premium payments and that gross margin improves from £184 per cow to £243 per cow, an increase of 32%. A further £42 per cow would be available if extensification premium could be claimed and this would increase the improvement in gross margin to 55%.

• At the other end of the scale the finisher of purchased calves is less likely to be satisfied although in theory this kind of enterprise should benefit more from lower grain prices. This type of enterprise is restricted by the 90-head limit per age group and so gains relatively little from the increase in beef special premium. Indeed, in the first year particularly, there may in practice be no increase because two generations of cattle are likely to be claimed in the first year, thus triggering the reference herd limits. This type of enterprise is also more likely to be restricted by stocking density and would usually be unable to claim extensification. The apparently high increases in beef special premium may encourage many smaller producers to purchase calves and thus drive up the initial buying-in price of calves which are usually sourced through the dairy herd for this type of enterprise. In addition, the delay in the cash flow from beef special premiums is another negative factor affecting finishers of cattle.

• To illustrate the possible effect of the reforms on an intensive finisher of purchased dairy type calves a gross margin comparison is set out below for a 100-head unit with no forage area. The major assumptions are that sale price falls by 15%, calf price rises by 10% and that feed costs decline by 20%.

Cereal-fed beef gross margin comparison
Pre (1992) and post (1995) reform – 100 head
1 ECU = £0.939052

	1992 £	1995 £
Output		
Sales	52,800	44,800
BSP	3,200	2,100*
(Calf purchase)	(12,000)	(13,200)
Total	44,000	33,700
Variable costs		
Concentrates	28,000	25,200
Miscellaneous	3,000	3,000
Total	31,000	28,200
Unit gross margin	**13,000**	**5,000**

*BSP payable on 15 LU (25 head)

For the 100-head example gross margin falls by some £7,500 or by 58%. The main problem for this type of beef enterprise is the loss of most compensation payments because there is no forage area.

• In between the extensive rearer and intensive finisher, there are the less intensive finishers of cattle, either from bought-in calves from the dairy herd or from purchased store cattle from the suckler herds. Many of these animals will already have had the first-age beef special premium claimed so that this should presumably cause a differential price in the store market, depending on the colour of the cattle passports. The temptation for many of these producers may be to take these cattle to at least 23 months of age so that they can claim the second-age beef special premium. In the past the "market" for this larger type of carcase has often been intervention and as this is less available, both in terms of reduced tonnage and reduced carcase weight, the marketing of this type of animal will become paramount.

• Finally, there is much speculation on the value of suckler cow quota. This is perhaps a little premature in that the outcome of the national reserve consultation is still not clear at the time of writing. It is generally thought that quota value will start at around £250 per cow, and on the basis of the amount of subsidy (including cow, calf and extensification and possibly HLCA) that attaches to a suckler cow, this could be on the low side. Also compared with the value of sheep quota, the suckler cow premium is more secure in that it is not a variable premium but a fixed amount of ECUs per cow per year. The premium increases over the first three years of the reform so that full value is not achieved until 1995. However, unless the fundamental economics of suckler beef production improves greatly, any substantial value placed on the cow quota is likely to detract from the value of the breeding animal itself.

Set out below is an example of the possible maximum subsidy attaching to an LFA suckler cow in 1995, assuming the January 1 1993 green pound conversion rate. This includes HLCA and extensification payments and assumes half the beef special premium (assuming 50% male calves).

Maximum subsidy per cow
£

SC premium	112
Extensification on SCP	28
HLCA	63
BSP (male calf @ 10 mths) £84 x 50%	42
Extensification on BSP £28 x 50%	14
Total	**259**

Those upland/hill farmers able to take advantage of these premiums may well be prepared to pay more than £250 for suckler cow quota. Cow quota outside the less favoured areas is likely to be worth considerably less as the HLCA payment and probably extensification would not be available.

E. SHEEPMEAT

Sheepmeat

17.1 Introduction

The 1992 reforms to the sheepmeat market were the least dramatic of
the three separate areas covered by this book. The reason for this is
that the whole of the common market in sheepmeat had been subject to
a substantial overhaul in 1989.[1] This overhaul involved the staged
withdrawal of the variable premium, introduction of a new scheme of
private storage aid and imposition of limits on the annual premium. The
1992 reforms have taken these limits on the annual premium one stage
further by imposing individual quotas on sheep producers wishing to
claim sheep annual premium. To obtain an overview and balanced
picture of how the market in sheepmeat is organised within the EC it is
necessary to consider the main support mechanisms involved and then
go on to consider the details of the 1992 reforms.

17.2 The common market

The common organisation of the market in sheepmeat and goatmeat
comprises both price and trading arrangements and covers sheep and
goats and their constituent components.[2]

17.3 Price and trading arrangements

The main support mechanisms are:

(i) private storage aid
(ii) import levies
(iii) export refunds
(iv) sheep annual premium

17.4 Definitions

17.4.1 Basic price
Central to the sheep annual premium scheme and private storage aid
scheme is the basic price. The basic price is the price which is fixed
annually within the farm price negotiations for the following market
year for fresh and chilled sheep carcasses.[3] It is fixed by reference to
various factors including:[4]

(a) the situation on the sheepmeat market during the current year
(b) the prospects for the production and consumption of sheepmeat
(c) sheepmeat production costs

---

1 Council Regulation 3013/89.
2 Article 1031 of Council Regulation 3013/89.
3 Article 3.1 of Council Regulation 3013/89.
4 Article 3.2 of Council Regulation 3013/89.

(d) the market situation in the other livestock product sectors, particularly the beef and veal sector

(e) past experience.

In short the Council is afforded a very wide measure of discretion and the Council also fixes seasonally adjusted basic prices taking into account normal seasonal variations of the community market in sheepmeat.[1]

For the 1992 marketing year the basic price was fixed at 422.95 ECUs per 100 kg carcass weight.[2] For 1993 the basic price is 418.53 ECUs per 100 kg carcase weight. However the basic price has been reduced in practice by a stabilizer mechanism. Under this mechanism if the size of the estimated community flock exceeds the maximum guaranteed level, currently fixed at 63,400,000 ewes,[3] then the basic price is reduced by a corresponding percentage.[4] The stabiliser for the EC in 1992 was 7%.

Since the stabiliser mechanism is applied on the basis of the estimated size of the community flock, it may need to be adjusted when the actual figures are known and before the final or definitive payment of sheep annual premium is made. If this cannot be achieved then the adjustment is carried forward into the next marketing year.[5] In 1992 the stabiliser was fixed provisionally at 7%.[6] The final figures were not available at the time of definitive payment being calculated[7] and therefore the adjustment, if any, is carried forward into 1993. The provisional stabiliser for 1993 is also 7%.

17.4.2   Weekly average weighted price

A weekly average weighted price is based on prices in representative markets within the community for standard quality carcasses. The prices are weighted according to volume of sheepmeat production in each area.[8] The weightings are:

Belgium	0.35%
Denmark	0.15%
Germany	4.76%
Spain	19.57%
France	15.90%
Greece	7.82%
Ireland	6.39%
Italy	5.06%
Luxembourg	–
Netherlands	2.29%
Portugal	2.37%
Great Britain	33.03%
Northern Ireland	2.31%
	100.00%

---

1 Article 3.2 of Council Regulation 3013/89.
2 Article 1 of Council Regulation 2063/92.
3 Article 8.1 of Council Regulation 3013/89.
4 Article 8.2 of Council Regulation 3013.89.
5 Article 8.2 of Council Regulation 3013/89.
6 Commission Regulation 1829/92.
7 Commission Regulation 502/93.
8 Article 4.1 of Council Regulation 3013/89.

Excluded from the weekly average weighted price calculation are light lambs. Light lambs are sheep from a flock utilized for milk production. All other sheep farmers are deemed to be producers of heavy lambs.[1]

17.4.3   Marketing year
The marketing year for sheepmeat begins on the first Monday in January and ends on the day preceding that date in the following year.[2]

17.5   Private storage aid

Intervention measures are authorised in the form of private storage aid schemes for carcasses and cuts of lamb.[3] Currently it is limited to carcasses and half carcasses less than one year old. Private storage aid has to be opened in a region if that region's market price falls below 70% of the basic price for two consecutive weeks.[4] Private storage aid schemes may be implemented in either of two sets of circumstances:

(i) when the weekly average weighted price[5] and the price in the region[6] fall below 90% of the seasonally adjusted[7] basic price.[8]

(ii) when the weekly average weighted price and the price in the region fall below 85% of the seasonally adjusted basic price and are likely to remain so.[9]

In the latter case the scheme must operate within the framework of a tendering procedure.

17.6   Import levies

Imports of live sheep and fresh chilled or frozen sheepmeat are subject to an import levy.[10] The levy is fixed each month by the Commission.[11]

The Community operates voluntary restraint agreements with most of the traditional supplying countries of sheepmeat. By far and away the most significant of these agreements is the one with New Zealand which permits in excess of 200,000 tonnes of sheepmeat to be imported into the Community. In return for entering into a voluntary restraint agreement no customs duty is imposed.

In the light of the voluntary restraint agreements the volume of sheepmeat imported into the Community and subject to import levies is minimal.

---

1 Article 4.3 of Council Regulation 3013/89.
2 Article 3.3 of Council Regulation 3013/89.
3 Article 6 of Council Regulation 3013/89.
4 Article 7.3 of Council Regulation 3013/89.
5 First paragraph of article 4.1 of Council Regulation 3013/89.
6 Second paragraph of Article 4.1 of Council Regulation 3013/89.
7 Article 3.2 of Council Regulation 3013/89.
8 Article 7.1 of Council Regulation 3013/89.
9 Article 7.2 of Council Regulation 3013/89.
10 Article 9 of Council Regulation 3013/89.
11 Article 10 of Council Regulation 3013/89.

17.7   Export refunds

Export refunds are permitted for exports to the extent necessary to enable the sheepmeat to be exported by producers without them losing out on community prices.[1]

17.8   Sheep annual premium

17.8.1   Calculation of sheep annual premium

The sheep annual premium is calculated as the difference between the basic price and the average of the weekly average weighted prices.[2] To this figure a co-efficient is applied which expresses for the whole Community the annual average sheep production of meat from heavy lambs per ewe producing such lambs, expressed per 100 kg carcass weight.[3]

For ewes producing light lambs the premium is calculated using the same loss of income calculation, but reducing the co-efficient to 80% of the co-efficient level for heavy lambs.[4]

Individual ewes are not classed as heavy or light but rather producers are classified as producers of ewes for light or heavy lambs. Provided a producer of ewes for light lambs can show that at least 40% of his lambs are fattened as heavy lambs he can claim the heavy premium in proportion to the number of lambs born on his holding and fattened as heavy carcasses.[5]

For goat meat producers in LFA's the premium is 70% of the premium for ewes payable to producers of heavy lambs.[6]

17.8.2   Cost of SAP

Since the sheep annual premium is a deficiency payment a prediction of future costs of the scheme is impossible. Under the scheme farmers in Great Britain received approximately £295,000,000 in 1991 and approximately £400,000,000 in 1992 after taking into account the various adjustments for currency fluctuations and LFA supplements.

17.8.3   Basis of payment

Sheep annual premiums are paid to producers according to the number of eligible ewes (and/or she goats) kept on their holding during the retention period.[7] An eligible ewe is any female of the ovine species which has lambed at least once or is at least one year old[8] by the end of

---

1 Article of 16 of Council Regulation 3013/89.
2 Article 5.1 of Council Regulation 3013/89.
3 Article 5.2 of Council Regulation 3013/89.
4 Article 5.3 of Council Regulation 3013/89 as amended by Article 1 of Council Regulation 2069/92.
5 Article 5.4 of Council Regulation 3013/89.
6 Article 5.5 of Council Regulation 3013/89.
7 Fifth paragraph of Article 5.6 of Council Regulation 3013/89.
8 Article 1.4 of Council Regulation 3493/90 as amended by Article 1 of Council Regulation 2070/92.

the retention period.[1] The regulations also define a holding as all the production units managed by the producer or made available to him and located in one member state.[2]

17.8.4   Application periods
A producer applying for sheep annual premium has to deliver his application to the competent authority within one of two periods:

(i) on or after November 15 and not later than December 15 in the preceding marketing year

(ii) on or after January 15 in the calendar year in which the marketing year commences and not later than February 20 in that calendar year.[3]

17.8.5   Retention period
The retention period of 100 days commences on the first day after the applicable application period. Thus, in relation to the first application period the retention period runs from December 16 to midnight on March 25 and in relation to the second application period from February 21 to midnight on May 31. The significance of having extended the definition of eligible ewe to encompass animals which have lambed or are one year old by the end of the retention period will be appreciated and is dealt with in more detail below.

17.8.6   Date of payment
The full amount of sheep annual premium must be paid by October 15 of the year following the marketing year.[4] The amount of sheep annual premium has to have been determined by March 31 of the year following the marketing year. In 1992 this occurred on March 4 1993.[5] For Great Britain the difference between the basic price modified by the stabilizer and the market prices in 1992 was found to be 116.35 ECUs per 100 kg carcass.[6] The co-efficient relevant to the variable premium for Great Britain was 16 kg which led to an overall premium payable per ewe for producers of heavy lamb of 18.61 ECUs. For light lambs the corresponding figure was 14.89 ECUs.[7]

The LFA supplement for heavy lambs was set at 7 ECUs per ewe[8] exceptionally for 1992. The normal rate is 5.5 ECUs.

There is a complex regulatory system for calculating and making advance payments. The Commission has to assess the foreseeable income loss for the entire marketing year and the foreseeable amount of the

---

1 Article 5.3 of Commission Regulation 3007/84 as amended by Commission Regulation 3204/92.
2 Article 1.3 of Council Regulation 3493/90.
3 Regulation 3(2) of The Sheep Annual Premium Regulations 1992.
4 Article 1 of Council Regulation 2069/92 amending Article 5 of Council Regulation 3013/89.
5 Commission Regulation 502/93.
6 Article 1 of Commission Regulation 502/93.
7 Article 3 of Commission Regulation 502/93.
8 Commission Regulation 363/93 and Article 4 of Commission Regulation 502/93.

premium. It has to do this before the end of each half-year and the Member States are allowed to pay their producers a half-yearly advance payment of 30% of the expected premium. In 1992 in the UK these initial advances were 5.67 ECUs (£4.51)[1] and 5.51 ECUs (£4.38)[2] respectively per ewe for producers of heavy lambs.

If the amount to be paid to producers is minimal it can be carried forward and added to premiums payable per ewe in the following year.[3]

If it should happen that the advance payments prove to exceed the amount of premium that would finally be paid in a marketing year the excess payment is deductible from payments made in the following year.[4]

The final sheep annual premiums payable in Great Britain for the 1992 marketing year will be as follows:

	Low Ground £	LFA £
First advance (paid August-November 1992)	4.51	8.88
Second advance (paid November-March 1993)	4.38	4.38
Final payment (expected April/May 1993)	8.59	10.79
Total	17.48	24.05

17.8.7   Producer/headage limits

The producer limit is commonly called the headage limit and is not to be confused with individual quotas. The headage limit restricts the premium paid at the full rate to producers in an LFA to 1,000 animals per producer and outside LFA's the limit for full rate payment is 500.[5] Claims in excess of these headage limits are paid at half rate.[6]

The limits apply individually to each producer even if he is a member of one or more producer groups. Thus a producer can only qualify once for the premium at the full rate within the limits.[7]

17.8.8   Producer

A sheepmeat producer is defined as an individual, whether a natural or legal person, who on a permanent basis, assumes the risks and/or organises the rearing of at least ten ewes within the territory of a single member state.[8] For these purposes the farmer is generally taken to be the owner of the flock. However, exceptions are envisaged where under the laws, customs or practices of a member state the farmer is not the owner of all or part of the flock but assumes the risks and/or organisation of the rearing of the flock.

---

1   Commission Regulation 1830/92.
2   Commission Regulation 3249/92.
3   Article 3 of Council Regulation 3493/90.
4   Article 4 of Council Regulation 3493/90.
5   Article 5.2 of Council Regulation 3013/89.
6   Article 5.7 of Council Regulation 3013/89.
7   Article 2.1 of Council Regulation 3493/90.
8   Article 1.1 of Council Regulation 3493/90.

Thus, the starting point is to determine who owns the flock. One goes on to see whether the owner assumes the risks and/or organises the rearing of the flock and whether he does so on a permanent basis. If no farmer meeting these criteria can be found one may in certain circumstances see whether the farmer could be some other person assuming the risks and/or organisation of the rearing. Quite apart from the risks of creating a tenancy under landlord and tenant law,[1] a so-called share farming arrangement which involved a fixed rate of return to the "farmer" may lead to problems since the farmer's real level of assumption of risk and involvement in organisation may be non-existent.

If a flock is owned by two or more persons the producer is deemed to be the person having the largest share of the sale of products from the flock.[2] There is no provision determining who is the producer where the share of the sale of products from the flock is equal between two or more owners.

Agisted sheep owned by a producer remain the producer's sheep for sheep annual premium purposes while the sheep are agisted although the producer has to identify the agister's holding in his premium application.[3]

The lessee of a wholly or partly leased flock of sheep is deemed to be the producer if he receives the income from the livestock products.[4] The producer limits apply to the whole of the flock belonging to the lessor and to the whole of the flock held by the lessee.[5] However, both lessor and lessee will have to identify the other's holding and the other's ewe numbers so as to avoid double counting.[6] Special arrangements for the National Trust in its capacity of lessor in the Lake District area provide that each lessee is subject to separate producer limits. These special terms have been obtained on the basis of the need to maintain environmental protection.[7]

There are special provisions where the shepherd of the flock is an employee of the producer (in accordance with the definition set out above), but is himself at the same time a producer in respect of part of the flock. To avoid double counting the producer limits apply to the whole flock belonging to the two producers so only 500 full rights could be claimed unless in an LFA when it would be 1,000. Furthermore, unless the two parts of the flock are identified separately both producers are jointly and severally liable to penalties applicable where less than the number of ewes declared are found on the holding upon inspection.[8]

Because of the special significance of LFAs there is the necessity to define who is to be a producer in a less favoured area. Obviously anyone farming exclusively in an LFA counts[9] but there are numerous complex

---

1 See section 1 of the Agricultural Holdings Act 1986.
2 Article 1 of Commission Regulation 2385/91.
3 Article 1.2 of Commission Regulation 2385/91.
4 First paragraph of Article 1.3 of Commission Regulation 2385/91.
5 Second paragraph of Article 1.3 of Commission Regulation 2385/91.
6 Third paragraph of Article 1.3 of Commission Regulation 2385/91.
7 Second recital to Commission Regulation 2385/91.
8 Article 4.4 of Commission Regulation 2385/91.
9 First paragraph of Article 2.2 of Council Regulation 3493/90.

factual situations that have arisen when a producer farms or has farmed partly in an LFA and partly outside it. The rule is that a producer whose holding has at least 50% of its agricultural area utilised for farming in an LFA is regarded as an LFA producer provided that the 50% minimum is used for sheep production. What is unclear is when land is to be regarded as used for sheep production. The concept of areas used for milk production is familiar territory for milk quota experts,[1] but sheep farming is likely often to involve more transient use of land. For instance, is land "used for sheep production" where sheep are used to graze the aftermath of a crop or to follow up after a dairy herd?

Particular problems are also emerging for farmers whose status in relation to LFA has altered since 1991. Allocation of quota, as we shall see later, is primarily based on the producer's status in the reference year of 1991. MAFF guidelines state that,

> Allocations have normally been based on your LFA/non-LFA status under the 1991 scheme. However, if your Regional Service Centre is aware that as a result of acquiring or disposing of land your LFA/non-LFA status changed between 1991 and 1992, it will have based your designation on the position under the 1992 scheme. If your position has changed between 1992 and 1993, or if you have any other query about your designation, you should contact your Regional Service Centre. Please note that normally no adjustment in LFA/non-LFA designation will be possible for changes which occurred after the 15 November 1992, the opening date for applications under the 1993 scheme.

So far, producers who have followed this advice and contacted their regional service centres have not been provided with answers and been told to wait. The EC regulations dealing with sheep quota make no reference to this problem which is illustrative of the difficulties that are encountered when non-land based quotas are issued which derive at least one of their characteristics from the nature of the land being farmed.

17.8.9   Producer groups

How to deal with producer groups in the sheep sector for premium purposes has given rise to an expanding mass of legislation. The first principle is that the headage limit applies individually to each of the member farmers of the group.

Producer groups are defined as any form of group, association or co-operation involving reciprocal rights and obligations between producers of sheepmeat. Associations the object of which is the joint rearing of a flock in such a manner that ownership of it cannot be attributed to its members individually are also considered to be producer groups, provided that it is established that those members personally assume the risks and/or the organisation of rearing.[2] A group includes partnerships, share farming agreements, associations or other forms of co-operation between producers and is thus a very wide definition intended to apply to the situation where a number of people farm together.

---

1   See *Puncknowle Farms Ltd* v *Kane* [1985] 272 EG 1283.
2   Article 1.2 of Council Regulation 3493/92.

As with the definition of producer the regulation looks to identify the real farmer involved in the commercial risk of the venture to qualify for payment of premium.

Producer groups are only entitled to submit one premium application which has to be signed by all the producers. All of the producers have to comply with the conditions relating to sheep annual premium and the group itself is liable to the penalties for non-compliance. The premium is paid directly to the group. The penalty for deliberately false and seriously negligent declarations is not just exclusion from premium for the year concerned but also for the following year.[1] This sanction cannot be avoided by producers leaving the group in the following year. It will apply to those producers individually wherever they go so long as they are producers.[2]

In August 1991[3] a host of anti-avoidance devices were introduced aimed at tightening up the workings of the headage limits. A less charitable view of the information that was sought from producers at that time was that governments and the Commission were arming themselves with the necessary information to impose quotas using 1991 as a reference year. In any event it became apparent that it would only be a matter of time before individual quotas were imposed based primarily on the information obtained in 1991 and this is indeed what has happened.

Because the problems arising from these anti-avoidance provisions are by no means all resolved and it is essential to understand them when considering the 1993 allocations of individual quotas to producer group members an outline of the measures is provided.

First and foremost, by August 31 1991, the formula for apportioning a producer group's assets and the number of ewes assigned to each producer had to be notified to the competent authority. Premium applications had to state the number of animals brought to the group by each producer[4] unless the nature of the group was such that the ownership of individual animals could not be assigned to each producer. In that case the constitution of the group had to contain some formula[5] for dealing with the group's assets upon the group being disbanded. The competent authority had to be told of the formula and thereafter the formula had to remain unaltered in subsequent market years. Thus the property rights of the group members *inter se* have been frozen unless a change could be justified on limited grounds. This could be seen as amounting to a significant intrusion into producer's rights of freedom. The formula can only be altered if the structure of the group undergoes "a substantial change" resulting from:

- new members joining or old members leaving, or

---

1 Article 6(6) of Commission Regulation 3007/84 as amended by Commission Regulation 1260/90.
2 Article 2 of Commission Regulation 2385/91.
3 Commission Regulation 2385/91.
4 First paragraph of Article 2(2) of Commission Regulation 2385/91.
5 Albeit implied under perhaps the Partnership Act 1890.

- a change of 10% or more in the apportionment of the member's assets as a whole.[1]

Both producer members who had an employer/employee relationship with another producer member or with the group[2] and producer members who did not contribute to the capital and labour of the enterprise and had no corresponding share of the profits were excluded from the headage limits.[3] There was a further anti-avoidance provision aimed at preventing new producer groups being set up by means of splitting up the flock and thereby obtaining for each producer increased headage limits.[4]

17.8.10   Records
A producer has to maintain a register showing:

(a) the dates on which female sheep put to the ram for the first time gave birth and the number of lambs produced
(b) the number and date of any sheep purchased, sold or otherwise disposed of, the name and address of the seller, buyer or other recipient or in the case of sheep purchased or sold at a livestock market, the name and address of the market
(c) in cases of losses of sheep the date the producer discovered the loss, the number lost and the circumstances of the loss

and then keep that register for three years.[5]

---

1   Article 2(2) of Commission Regulation 2385/91 as amended by Commission Regulation 3676/91.
2   Article 2.3(a) of Commission Regulation 2385/91 as amended by Commission Regulation 3676/91.
3   Article 2.3 of Commission Regulation 2385/91.
4   Article 2.4 of Commission Regulation 2385/91 as amended by Commission Regulation 3676/91.
5   Regulation 4 of The Sheep Annual Premium Regulations 1992.

The 1992 reforms to sheep annual premium

18.1   Introduction

Since 1989 the number of claims to sheep annual premium that can be made by a producer has been limited by a ceiling on full rights claims of 1,000 in LFAs and 500 in other areas with no limit to the number of half rights thereafter. These are called headage limits. Broadly, all that a producer needed to do to obtain the sheep annual premiums was to be in possession of an eligible ewe for the requisite period of time and apply correctly. The 1992 reforms limit producers' rights to claim sheep annual premium by the imposition of individual limits based on the number of claims made in 1991. From 1993 onwards sheep annual premium will only be paid to producers holding an adequate number of premium rights (sheep quota).[1] This quota is in addition to the existing headage limits so that, for example, a producer in a non-LFA with a quota of 750 and with 800 eligible ewes would receive 500 full premium rights and 250 half premium rights.

18.2   Straightforward allocations

If a producer was granted premium in respect of the 1991 marketing year and applied for premium in the 1992 marketing year then he is entitled to sheep annual premium quota.[2] His quota of premium rights is the number which he applied for in 1991.[3] Producers applying for premium in 1992 who have taken over or inherited a holding from another producer who claimed the premium in 1991 but ceased farming in 1992 receive the quota which the latter would have received had he continued farming in 1992.[4]

The minimum size of quota is 10 for allocation purposes[5] and only whole numbers are used.[6]

The final amount of the quota is calculated after application of a national co-efficient. The national co-efficient represents the ratio between the total number of eligible ewes at the beginning of either the 1989, 1990 or 1991 marketing years and the total number of eligible ewes for the 1991 marketing year.[7] In October 1992 Great Britain chose a reference year of 1990 as this gave a co-efficient of more than one. Because each member state has to reduce each individual producer's quota to make provision for a national reserve[8] the aim was to be able

---

1 Article 5 of Council Regulation 3013/89 as amended by Council Regulation 2069/92.
2 Article 5a.1 of Council Regulation 3013/89 as amended by Council Regulation 2069/92.
3 Article 5a.1 and Article 5a4(a) of Council Regulation 3013/89 as amended by Council Regulation 2069/92.
4 Article 12 of Commission Regulation 3567/92.
5 Article 2.1 of Commission Regulation 3567/92.
6 Article 14 of Commission Regulation 3567/92.
7 Article 5a.5 of Council Regulation 3013/89 as amended by Council Regulation 2069/92.
8 Article 5b of Council Regulation 3013/89 as amended by Council Regulation 2069/92.

to end up allocating quotas based on 1991 eligible ewe numbers.[1]

18.3   Other allocations

18.3.1   Natural circumstances

Where there are natural circumstances which resulted in non-payment or reduced payment in 1991 (marketing year) the allocation of quota is based on the number of animals for which claims were made in the most recent marketing year.[2]

The most recent marketing year would tend to indicate 1992, but contrary to expectations it in fact means the year prior to 1991 in which the natural circumstances did not obtain.[3]

Natural circumstances in this context are defined. Producers can only have their quotas adjusted if their payments of sheep annual premium under the 1991 scheme were reduced due to:

- natural circumstances relating to the life of the flock which were notified to the competent authority in writing within ten days of the producer having been aware of them; or
- a serious natural disaster which had a major effect on their holding; or
- the accidental destruction of their fodder stocks or of their facilities intended for the rearing of their flock; or
- a disease which led to the slaughter of at least half of their flock on veterinary advice.[4]

These losses leading to a reduction of claims in 1991 had to have occurred either before they submitted a claim or before the April 24 1991 deadline which existed for 1991 sheep annual premium claim applications

18.3.2   Penalised producers

If a producer was subject to penalties that resulted in non-payment or reduced payment of the premium in 1991 then the quota allocation is based on the actual number of animals discovered when the check giving rise to the penalties was carried out. It is not clear whether this provision is wide enough to cover the position of a producer who failed to lodge any application at all or who lodged an application but so late that no check on animal numbers was ever carried out. It is anticipated that at least the latter will be covered by this provision and will receive quota but the former will have to rely on the national reserve.[5]

---

1   Article 5a.1 of Council Regulation 3013/89 as amended by Council Regulation 2069/92.
2   Article 5a.2 of Council Regulation 3013/89 as amended by Council Regulation 2069/92.
3   Article 3 of Commission Regulation 3567/92.
4   Article 3(b) of Commission Regulation 3567/92.
5   Articles 5a.2 and 5b.2(c) of Council Regulation 3013/89 as amended by Council Regulation 2069/92.

18.3.3 Additional premium rights

A producer who during 1991 participated in a Community extensification programme[1] may apply at the end of that programme for additional quota amounting to the difference between the number of sheep annual premium rights granted in 1991 and the number of sheep annual premium rights granted in the year before he entered into the Community extensification programme.[2]

However, additional quota cannot be transferred or leased in the three following years and if the producer does not use all of his rights during the three following years he loses the average number of rights not used to the national reserve.[3]

18.4 Allocations from the national reserves

18.4.1 Setting up

Member States are obliged to set up an initial national reserve consisting of between one and three percent of the total quota in the Member State. Deductions for producers' quotas brought about by the siphon on transfers without holdings also go to the national reserve.[4]

The UK has opted for a national reserve of 1.6% of its total quota being the difference in ewe numbers between 1990 (the chosen year) and 1991 (the year on which allocation was based).

It is estimated that the amount of quota made available from the national reserve in 1993 will be around 320,000 premium rights.

18.4.2 LFAs

Member States have to set up an additional national reserve equal to 1% of the quota in LFAs of the Member State and this quota can only be allocated to producers in LFA.[5] This LFA reserve will be about 130,000 premium rights.

18.4.3 Allocations

Member States have to use their national reserves for granting quota, as long as there is sufficient quota, to the following categories of producer[6]:

(i) producers who applied for premium prior to 1992 and who can show that the imposition of a quota would jeopardise the viability of their holdings, taking into consideration the implementation of an investment programme drawn up before January 1 1993;[7]

(ii) producers whose 1991 premium applications did not reflect their true situation due to exceptional circumstances. Producers true situations

---

1 Pursuant to Council Regulation 797/85.
2 Article 12.3 of Commission Regulation 3567/92.
3 Article 12.3 of Commission Regulation 3567/92.
4 Article 5b.1 of Council Regulation 3013/89 as amended by Council Regulation 2069/92.
5 Article 5b.3 of Council Regulation 3013/89 as amended by Council Regulation 2069/92.
6 Article 5b.2 of Council Regulation 3013/89 as amended by Council Regulation 2069/92.
7 Article 5b.2(a) of Council Regulation 3013/89 as amended by Council Regulation 2069/92.

are ascertained by reference to previous marketing years;[1]

(iii) producers who regularly submitted an application for premium but who did not do so in 1991. Such producers would include those who omitted to submit any application in 1991 but it is not clear whether producers who submitted an application but so late that no premium was paid have to rely on the national reserve or can obtain quota otherwise;[2]

(iv) new entrants in the sense of producers applying for sheep annual premium for the first time in 1993 and subsequent years;[3]

(v) producers acquiring part of an area used for sheep production;[4]

(vi) producers who obtained sheep annual premium in 1991 but did not apply in 1992 but who also continued to produce.[5]

Exceptionally a producer who continues producing in 1992 but did not apply for sheep annual premium in that year is eligible to receive quota from the national reserve.[6]

18.4.4   Restrictions on national reserve quota

The producer who obtains his quota free of charge from the national reserve cannot transfer or lease his quota for the three following marketing years.[7] If such a producer does not utilise all of his quota during the three following years the average number of rights not used by him over those three years is returned to the national reserve.[8]

18.4.5   Applications

Applications for quota from the national reserve can be made in accordance with rules laid down by Member States but applications have to have been made by June 30 1993 at the latest.[9]

18.5   Producer groups

As with the headage limits imposed in 1989 the quota allocation of the group is limited to the sum of the individual member's quota rights.[10] The quota allocations are given to the individual members of the group.[11] When the premium is paid to the group the quota is based on the sum of the individual members quota and changes in the membership of the group are taken into account. In this way the system is intended to operate by initially linking premium rights (quota) to the producer owning or having the right to own the corresponding eligible

---

1   Article 5b.2(b) of Council Regulation 3013/89 as amended by Council Regulation 2069/92.
2   Article 5a.2 of Council Regulation 3013/89 as amended by Council Regulation 2069/92.
3   Article 5b.2(d) of Council Regulation 3013/89 as amended by Council Regulation 2069/92.
4   Article 5b.2(e) of Council Regulation 3013/89 as amended by Council Regulation 2069/92.
5   Article 12.2 of Commission Regulation 3567/92.
6   Article 12.2 of Commission Regulation 3567/92.
7   Article 6.1(a) of Commission Regulation 3567/92.
8   Article 6.1(b) of Commission Regulation 3567/92.
9   Article 12.4 of Commission Regulation 3567/92.
10 Article 5a.3 of Council Regulation 3013/89 as amended by Council Regulation 2069/92.
11 Article 5a.3 of Council Regulation 3013/89 as amended by Council Regulation 2069/92.

ewes and leaving individuals relatively free to move with both sheep and quota.

It is at this point that the relevance of the detailed provisions surrounding the imposition of the producer limits and the anti-avoidance measures referred to in the previous chapter can be seen.

The individual members' quotas are worked out according to the following rules:

(i) The formula notified to the competent authority in the 1991 group claim form.

It will be recalled from the previous chapter that the formula was either according to the individual ownership of the flock or the ownership of the flock in accordance with the rules of disbandment of the group according to the group's constitution.[1]

(ii) Only groups whose claims exceeded the headage limit had to provide the information so for other groups the individual quotas are worked out according to the breakdown of flock ownership or apportionment on the group's 1992 claim form.[2]

If the producer group was set up during 1992 sheep annual premium is paid to the group on the basis of individual members' quotas based on the number of premiums granted to the producer members in 1991. Thereafter, for 1993, each individual producer member is awarded his own quota. If the group is unable to determine the ownership of the flock between individual members then the apportionment formula that will have been notified by the group in its 1992 application is applied to allocate quota to individual members.[3]

18.6   Notification of quota

Each producer had to be told what his quota is no later than 15 days before the end of the period laid down by Member States for submission of premium applications in 1993.[4] In the UK the application periods for 1993 sheep annual premium were:

(a) November 15 1992 to December 15 1992
(b) January 15 1993 to February 20 1993[5]

The notification had to state the number of full and half premium rights.[6]

If a Member State could not determine the precise number of rights to be allocated due to some sort of dispute a provisional allocation was

---

1   Article 5a.3(a) of Council Regulation 3013/89 as amended by Council Regulation 2069/92.
2   Article 5a.3(b) of Council Regulation 3013/89 as amended by Council Regulation 2069/92.
3   Article 2.2 of Commission Regulation 3567/92.
4   Article 2.3 of Commission Regulation 3567/92.
5   Regulation 3(2) of The Sheep Annual Premium Regulations 1992 SI No. 2677.
6   Article 2.3 of Commission Regulation 3567/92.

made.[1] Where there was a fraudulent application in 1991 it will be recalled that one of the sanctions is no entitlement to premium in the following year.[2] Nevertheless such producers received a quota based on the number of animals found when the check was carried out in 1991.[3]

18.7   Use of quota

Save in exceptional cases if the producer does not make use of at least 50% of his quota, by either claiming sheep annual premium himself or leasing his quota, during two consecutive years then the amount not used in the second year has to be transferred to the national reserve.[4] However, if he leases his quota it will be seen that he sets the clock running against himself in another context.

18.8   Transfers

A producer is able to transfer his premium rights (quota). If he transfers all of his quota to a person who takes over his holding the transfer is free from a siphon to the national reserve.[5] However, if he transfers either all or part of his premium rights without his holding then a maximum of 15% of the quota is siphoned to the national reserve, without compensation to the producer, for distribution free of charge to new entrants or other priority producers.[6] However, the number of rights transferred can never be less than one.[7]

Producers who farm only on publicly or collectively owned land and who decide to stop using that land for grazing[8] and transfer all their rights to another producer are exempt from the siphon.[9]

Member States can provide that transfers of quota without holdings and leases of quota should take place via the national reserve,[10] but this has not happened in the UK.

18.9   Minimum size of partial transfers/leases

Where a producer does not transfer all of his quota the minimum number of premium rights that may be transferred are:[11]

* 10% of the number representing the size of the flock of eligible

---

1 Article 2.3 of Commission Regulation 3567/92.
2 Article 6(6) of Commission Regulation 3007/84 as amended.
3 Article 2.3 of Commission Regulation 3567/92.
4 Article 6(2) of Commission Regulation 3567/92.
5 Article 5a.4(b) of Council Regulation 3013/89 as amended by Council Regulation 2069/92.
6 Article 5a.4(b) and Article 5b2 of Council Regulation 3013/89 as amended by Council Regulation 2069/92.
7 Article 7.3 of Commission Regulation 3567/92.
8 Compare the more onerous obligation of having to permanently give up farming in the suckler cow premium regime.
9 Article 10 of Commission Regulation 3567/92.
10 Article 11 of Commission Regulation 3567/92.
11 Article 5a.4(a) of Council Regulation 3013/89 as amended by Council Regulation 2069/92.

animals, with a maximum of 50, if a producer has 50 or more premium rights;

- five premium rights if the producer has between 20 and 49 premium rights;
- one premium right if the producer has less than 20 premium rights.[1]

Thus, if the number of premium rights held exceeds 500 then the minimum size of quota transfer is 50 and if the number of premium rights held is between 50 and 499 it is 10% of the quota.

The same minimum size rules apply to leases of quota.[2]

18.10 Ring fences

Member States are bound to take measures to avoid quota moving from sensitive zones or regions where sheep production is especially important for the local economy.[3] As with suckler cow premium quota a consultation period as to ring fencing and other matters was commenced on January 25 1993 until February 15 1993 and it is widely believed that the ring fenced areas will be:

(i)   the lowlands in Great Britain;
(ii) English LFA;
(iii) Welsh LFA;
(iv) Scottish LFA;
(v)   Scottish highlands and islands;
(vi) Northern Irish LFA;
(vii) Northern Irish lowlands.

National reserves are also likely to be ring fenced in the same way.

18.11 Leasing

A producer is entitled to lease out part of his quota which he does not intend to use but over a period of five years from first leasing the producer must, unless he transfers his quota, use all his quota himself in at least two consecutive marketing years.[4] Thus careful consideration should be given to leasing before it is undertaken because of the need to resume full production for the two following years and if less than 50% of the producer's quota is going to remain unutilized it might, in certain circumstances, be more sensible for the producer not to lease at all. This is because subsequent attempts at leasing where full production over two consecutive years within five has not taken place will be invalidated.[5]

---

1   Article 7.1 of Commission Regulation 3567/92.
2   Article 7.4 of Commission Regulation 3567/92.
3   Article 5a.4(c) of Council Regulation 3013/89 as amended by Council Regulation 2069/92.
4   Article 5a4(d) of Council Regulation 3013/89 as amended by Council Regulation 2069/92.
5   Articles 7.4 of Commission Regulation 3567/92.

MAFF have also made it clear that they will not process leases of quota within the five-year period from the leasing if it is clear that the producer will not be able to comply with the requirement to fully utilise the quota in at least two consecutive years.[1]

There is the possibility of Member States implementing limited exceptions for producers who were participating in the extensification programme and who therefore may have difficulties in the initial years after ceasing such a programme in fully utilising their quota.[2]

18.12　Transfers/leases and headage limits

The producer who is either the transferee or lessee of quota has the transferred or leased quota added to his original allocation but he is still subject to the headage limit and thus the number of full rights that he can obtain is a maximum of 1,000 in LFA and 500 in non-LFA. Thereafter, his rights acquired can only be 50% rights.[3] Thus, where 50% rights are transferred or leased by a producer and the transferee or lessee continues to fall short of the headage limit applicable to him then the rights acquired are divided by two and they become full premium rights. Equally where a producer transfers or leases full premium rights to another producer who exceeds his headage limit the number of rights acquired is doubled and they become 50% rights.[4]

18.13　Formalities

No transfer or lease of quota is effective until it has been notified to the Member State's competent authority (in England this is MAFF) by both parties to the transaction.[5]

Member States have to set a deadline for notifying transfers and leases. This deadline cannot expire more than two months before the first date of the first application period for sheep annual premium. Because of implementation difficulties in 1993 Member States can set their own notification deadlines.[6]

Both parties to transfers and leases of quota have to be informed of their revised quota levels for that year before the beginning of the first application period for sheep annual premium claims. The notification must tell them the division between their full and 50% premium rights.[7]

As with allocations, only whole numbers of quota are used and where a calculation gives rise to something other than a whole number the nearest whole number is used. When the figure is half way between two whole numbers the higher whole number is used.[8]

1　MAFF Explanatory Booklet para 43.
2　Article 7.4 of Commission Regulation 3567/92.
3　Article 5a.4(e) of Council Regulation 3013/89 as amended by Council Regulation 2069/92.
4　Article 8 of Commission Regulation 3567/92.
5　Article 7.2 of Commission Regulation 3567/92.
6　Article 7.2 of Commission Regulation 3567/92.
7　Article 9 of Commission Regulation 3567/92.
8　Article 14 of Commission Regulation 3567/92.

18.14　Landlord and tenant

There are provisions[1] enabling Member States to resolve specific problems linked to the transfer of quota, or actions having equivalent effect, by producers who do not own the land which constitutes their holding. However, any measures that a Member State implements have to be limited to dealing with the problems of introducing quotas linked to producers and not land and the measures must represent the principle of quota going with producers and not being linked to land. As with suckler cow premium quota the difficulty in the UK has been to achieve any sort of consensus about whether there were any specific problems and the shape of any problems identified. All the EC Regulations do is recognise that such problems may exist. As with suckler cow quota the authors' views are that in some circumstances problems do already exist. Take for example the case of a tenant on a hill farm who was a producer on that holding in 1991 and 1992 for the purposes of sheep annual premium and was therefore allocated ewe quota. If that tenant has since moved holding he is quite entitled under the EC legislation to take that quota with him, although up to 15% will be surrendered to the national reserve. The tenant is content because he has most of the newly created asset and can carry on farming elsewhere. The landlord on the other hand has a hill farm, very likely not suited to production other than sheep, but with no quota. What is that land worth to another tenant who now has to own both ewes and quota to practise any form of economic farming on that holding? The tenant is surely going to offer a lower rent, and the landlord will claim the introduction of quotas has resulted in a substantial reduction in the capital value of his land. It has been suggested that landlords may try to make cases against departing tenants for dilapidations, but there may be considerable legal problems depending upon the terms of the lease.

At one point the draft EC Regulations mentioned the word "compensation" in relation to this recognised problem, but the final regulation refers only to "appropriate transitional measures with a view to finding equitable solutions to problems". All that the Government have suggested so far is that landlords finding themselves in this position will be given priority in allocations of quota from the national reserve. At the same time the suggestion is that the siphon for transferring quota away from holdings should be set at the maximum 15% level, presumably to discourage such transfers and to put more quota into the reserve to be allocated to landlords and new tenants who have no quota. However, in the consultation document, this category of producer is 3(b) behind six other categories with higher priority. While the tenant waits for an allocation he must continue to farm, and would almost certainly have to be prepared to lease quota for 1993 sheep annual premium. The market rate appears to be around £11 per ewe for leased Scottish LFA sheep quota which is a level higher than most tenants would pay in

---

1　Article 5a.4(f) of Council Regulation 3013/89 as amended by Council Regulation 2069/92 and Article 13 of Commission Regulation 3567/92.

annual rent per ewe. For this situation it would be very surprising if rents and therefore land values were not affected.

The EC legislation appears to imply that these problems are only temporary and that they apply only to leases existing at the time of the introduction of quotas. However, if quota attaches to producers the landlord will always be in the position of having to try to persuade the tenant to leave quota behind, and there must inevitably be a financial penalty to the landlord in this situation.

Nor are these problems likely to be related only to hill farms. A low ground sheep unit which has been in grass for a number of years will not be eligible to be registered under IACS as arable land, and therefore the alternative uses for such land have become limited with the advent of the 1992 CAP reforms. Such land left without quotas by departing tenants is likely to suffer a fall in value.

18.15   Implications for the sheep sector

The reforms have no direct impact on market prices for sheepmeat so that the implications are concerned only with the changes arising from the introduction of quota.

The definition of "eligible ewe" was changed, almost unnoticed for a time, to a female sheep "having lambed at least once or aged at least one year by the end of the retention period". This change could have a fundamental effect on the sheep industry because sheep annual premium can now be claimed on:

- old cast ewes that are not put to the tup, probably claimed in the first application period and retained until March 25 and then sold fat
- ewe lambs/hoggs kept for breeding which would in nearly every case be over a year old by the end of the retention period for the second application period, ie May 31.

Therefore, unless application/retention periods are adjusted radically or the definition changed again, there is almost certainly going to be an increased demand for quota from the following categories of producer:

- low ground, possibly arable, farms purchasing old ewes in the cast sales and feeding for sale in the normally high price period in April/May
- hill farmers who normally keep their own replacements. They will either buy or lease in the extra quota making no change to their farming practice, but increase their subsidy take, or take the opportunity to reduce stock numbers and merely reduce ewes, but without reducing their subsidy take.

Also producers who have temporarily gone out of breeding sheep production but who want to hold on to their quotas can do this without falling foul of the penalties for not using ewe quota by a combination of leasing and the setting up of an old ewe fattening enterprise for two consecutive years in five. Thus they avoid having to employ a specialist lambing shepherd.

None of these changes in sheep farming practice need worry the Commission because with a quota cap on ewe numbers all the above enterprises would result in fewer lambs and therefore in theory less expenditure on the sheep regime. The number of sheep annual premium claims would remain the same, but with fewer lambs, the average market price for lambs in the Community should rise and therefore the level of sheep annual premium payments should fall.

18.16   Value of ewe quota

Ewe quotas have been trading even before the legislation is in place to allow the transfer to be legally effective. Scottish LFA quota has been sold subject to final transfer at up to £45 per ewe. On the basis of the total 1992 LFA sheep annual premium of £24 it is on the face of it perhaps surprising that prices have not been higher. In fact little sale of quota has taken place, with most ewe quota on offer for leasing at about £9 – £11 per ewe for LFA and £6 – £8 per ewe for non-LFA.

No doubt purchasers are well aware that 1992 sheep annual premium levels are unlikely to be so high again, particularly in the LFAs. The extra 1.5 ECUs to LFAs will not occur again and the green pound could have revalued by January 1994 to reduce the value to UK producers of sheep annual premium. Also lamb prices have been very strong not just in the UK but throughout the Community in early 1993 and are expected to stay well above 1992 levels. All this may result in a much lower level of sheep annual premium for the 1993 marketing year and beyond. In fact it is well to remember that sheep annual premium is a "variable" premium, and in theory could lose all its value even without a political decision to cancel it.

This all makes predicting values difficult as there is undoubtedly a fairly strong demand for quota at present, especially in the LFAs – no doubt partly stimulated by the points made above. What is fairly certain is that values will vary in the seven different zones and that at present demand in the Great Britain lowland ring fence does not appear to be particularly strong.

Taxation of livestock premiums and quotas

19   Livestock premiums

Livestock premiums have of course been available for some while past. The new CAP regulations simply impose a quota system for eligibility for those premiums.

Premiums will form part of the trading receipts of the farming business and will be taken into account in computing the trading profit brought into account for income or corporation tax.

Suckler cow premium, beef special premium and ewe premium are all paid on specific dates against proof that the relevant number of animals were kept on the initial qualifying day and for the relevant qualifying period thereafter.

The date of receipt bears no necessary relation to the date of disposal of the beast in question – and indeed there is no requirement for sale in any case.

Although no official guidance has been published by the Revenue it is most likely that premium will fall to be taxed on a receipts basis – that is that they will be brought into account for tax for the period during which the premium was actually received.

Capital gains tax

The right to quota in any case where that right can be bought or sold will be treated as a capital asset for capital gains tax purposes.

The Revenue view is set out in a Budget release dated March 16 1993 in the following terms:

> The Chancellor proposes in his budget to add new EC agricultural quotas for the premium given to producers of ewes and suckler cows to the list of assets which qualify for capital gains tax rollover relief. In addition he proposes a general power to add by Treasury order to the list of assets which qualify for rollover relief.
>
> The Chancellor's proposals recognise the fact that since quota can be capital assets of farming trades rollover relief should be available for them.
>
> The changes will apply to acquisitions and disposals on or after 1 January 1993.

It is anticipated that this change will be given statutory effect by enlarging the relevant classes of assets for the purposes of rollover relief as set out in section 155 of the Taxation of Capital Gains Act 1992.

F. INTEGRATED ADMINISTRATION AND CONTROL SYSTEM (IACS)

Integrated Administration and Control System (IACS)

20.1 Introduction

Member States have to take the measures necessary to satisfy themselves that transactions financed by the European Agriculture Guidance Guarantee Fund (EAGGF) are actually carried out and are executed correctly.[1] With the advent of direct aid to producers there is a need[2] for an Integrated Administration and Control System (IACS) without which all scope for control over spending would be lost. IACS applies to:[3]

(i)   the aid schemes for arable crops[4]
(ii) the beef special premium and suckler cow premium schemes for beef and veal[5]
(iii) the premium scheme for sheep meat and goat meat[6]
(iv) specific measures for mountain farms and farms in less favoured areas.[7] In the UK this is the Hill Livestock Compensatory Allowance Scheme (HLCAS).[8]

The theory is that this highly complex system will result in more effective administration of the CAP but the Council of Ministers recognised that the system involved introducing a "high additional budgetary burden".[9] This is certain and it must also be certain that IACS introduces significant additional burdens on producers in terms of paperwork and formalities and on governments in setting up the additional bureaucracy.

The new system involves:

* establishment of a computerised database
* an ID system for each agricultural parcel covered by an application for aid under the arable, sheep, beef and hill livestock schemes
* identifying and registering animals
* each farmer submitting detailed information about his holding each year
* an integrated system for checking and inspection.

The system has been likened to the Doomsday Book and will eventually contain a record of virtually all arable and forage parcels. It is clear that our own Minister of Agriculture has become alarmed at the volume of bureaucracy involved and the scale of the imposition on farmers.

---

1 Article 8 of Council Regulation 729/70.
2 An obligation under Article 1 of Council Regulation 3508/92.
3 Article 1 of Council Regulation 3508/92.
4 Council Regulation 1765/92.
5 Articles 4(a) to (h) of Council Regulation 805/68 as amended.
6 Council Regulation 3013/89.
7 Council Regulation 2328/91.
8 The Hill Livestock (Compensatory Allowance) Regulations 1992.
9 Twelfth Recital of Council Regulation 3508/92.

IACS is to be implemented in two stages. The first stage came into effect on February 1 1993. The full system has to be operative by January 1 1996.

20.2   Definitions

For purposes of the integrated system the following definitions are provided:[1]

- *Farmer* means an individual agricultural producer, whether a natural or legal person or a group of legal or natural persons, whatever legal status is granted the group and its members by national law, whose holding is within the Community territory
- *Holding* means all the production units managed by a farmer situated within the same Member State's territory
- *Agricultural parcel* means a continuous area of land on which a single crop is raised by a single farmer.

The definition of farmer is similar to the definition of producer in other regimes and plainly wide enough to embrace partnerships, share farming agreements and any other UK law concepts involving more than one person in farming. Individual members of producer groups will have to be identified accurately. The definition of farmer and holding taken in conjunction with each other show that the farmer must be the producer who actually farms the land and manages it. MAFF guidance[2] states that each separate business farming land has to submit a separate IACS form. The question that this raises is whether one individual with separate businesses farming the land has to submit separate IACS forms. MAFF appear to think so. This may have important practical implications particularly when considering the number of claims that may be made for beef special premium. But how separate must these businesses be? MAFF suggest[3] that they will be looking to discover separate farm plans and accounts and independence of decision making. Businesses jointly run as part of a single enterprise or which take management decisions in common have to submit one IACS form.

Share farming arrangements raise a particular problem because it is of the essence of the arrangement that both "farmer" and "contractor" maintain separate businesses albeit based on the same farm. Apparently only one IACS form should be submitted by one of the parties authorised in writing by the other.

Holding is the common definition applied in a number of EC regimes. All the land farmed by a farmer within the UK is regarded as a single unit and MAFF require only a single IACS form covering all farms.[4] Where holdings have been created or split up specifically to avoid the

---

1   Article 1.4 of Council Regulation 3508/92.
2   MAFF Explanatory Booklet para 134.
3   MAFF Explanatory Booklet para 134.
4   MAFF Explanatory Booklet para 11.

limits on eligibility for premiums or land set-aside requirements Member States have to take the necessary measures to ensure that such schemes are thwarted.[1] In the UK this has been done by requiring farmers to disclose in their IACS forms any other agricultural businesses in which they have a significant interest. Instances of significant interests are given[2] and these include partner and major shareholder. Minor shareholdings do not apparently have to be disclosed. Whether the words "major" and "minor" equate to majority and minority may be a matter for debate.

The concept of an agricultural parcel is new. The continuous area of land indicates that an agricultural parcel does not necessarily equate to a field and may be more or less than a field. However, only one crop can be grown on an agricultural parcel and a parcel can only be farmed by one farmer. If the area for which compensatory payment is sought contains trees due allowance has to be made for them.[3] However, a parcel of land used for crop production and containing trees remains a parcel so long as the trees do not effect the cultivation of the crop.[4]

20.3   Components of the integrated system

The components of the integrated system are:

(a) a computerised database
(b) an alphanumeric identification system for agricultural parcels
(c) an alphanumeric system for the identification and registration of animals
(d) aid applications
(e) an integrated control system.[5]

20.3.1   A computerised database
A computerised database which records for each holding the information from the aid applications going back three years.[6]

20.3.2   Alphanumeric identification and registration of land
Alphanumeric means by reference to letters and numbers. The alphanumeric identification system for agricultural parcels has to be established on the basis of land registry maps and documents, other cartographic evidence or aerial photographs or satellite pictures or similar references.[7] From this, one infers that once a parcel has been identified it has a degree of permanence on the ground whereas the definition of agricultural parcel is much vaguer. There appears to be no reason why one field, if of sufficient size, should not constitute several

---

1 Article 2.2 of Commission Regulation 3887/92.
2 MAFF Explanatory Booklet para 82.
3 Article 4.2 of Commission Regulation 2780/92.
4 Article 2.1(a) of Commission Regulation 3887/92.
5 Article 2 of Council Regulation 3508/92.
6 Article 3 of Council Regulation 3508/92.
7 Article 4 of Council Regulation 3508/92.

different parcels of varying size in different configurations each year. The computerised database in the UK has been set up on the basis that different crops may be grown on parts of one field. Each crop area then becomes a part parcel. The minimum field size on which aid can be claimed is 0.1 ha (unless it is used for seed production or research in which case it is 0.01 ha).[1]

20.3.3   The alphanumeric identification and registration of animals

The alphanumeric identification and registration of animals system is to be set up in accordance with Articles 4, 5, 6 and 8 of Directive 92/102/EEC.[2] This provides for a comprehensive identification and registration system of bovine and porcine animals both on holdings and at all times when moved thereafter. Eartags with alphanumeric code are the chosen method of identifying bovines. The system extends to animals imported or exported within the community and all such animals entering the community. Sheep do not have to be identified while on a holding but registers of sheep numbers kept on the holding have to be maintained. When moved off a holding individual identification is not required but marking with ear tag or tattoo is required to enable the holding from which it has come to be identified. Member States were required to implement this directive by February 1 1993. In the UK this directive has been implemented in respect of bovine animals by the Bovine Animals (Identification, Marking and Breeding Records) (Amendment) Order 1993.[3] The detail and level of formality required are considerable administrative impositions. The Order requires records to be kept of the birth or death of each bovine animal and the number of bovine animals kept on the holding and requires that the local Animal Health Office be notified of the name and address of the owner or occupier of a holding on which bovine animals are kept. The farm stock book has to record the following particulars:

Birth or Death	Date	Breed	Sex	Approved Identification	Approved Identification of Dam (where birth)	Total No of bovine animals on holding

Births in the dairy herd have to be recorded within 36 hours and other births within seven days.

20.3.4   Aid applications

To be eligible for aid under any one or more of the community schemes covered by IACS a farmer has to submit an area aid application form annually within the first three months of the year except for 1993 when the May 15 is set as the deadline.[4] There is some flexibility if a Member

---

1   MAFF Explanatory Booklet para 131.
2   Article 5 of Council Regulation 3508/92.
3   SI 1993 No 503 amending the Bovine Animals (Identification, Marking and Breeding Records) Order 1990.
4   Article 6.2 of Council Regulation 3508/92.

State can justify a later date. After the first year applicants may only have to submit a form showing changes from the previous year.[1] Amendments to the application can be made if received before May 15.[2]

The application must specify the agricultural parcels which includes forage crops and parcels set-aside and laid fallow. The application also has to give any other information required by either the Community or by a Member State.[3] The area and location of each parcel has to be provided by the applicant so that the land can be alphanumerically identified.[4] Documents accompanying the aid application are deemed to be part of the application.[5] This included maps in the 1993 application.

Farmers whose only application for aid is not linked directly to agricultural area can be exempted from the obligation to make the area aid application.[6]

Apart from having to submit the area aid application if a farmer wants to claim any of the aids covered by IACS, he must also submit one or more animal aid applications if he wants to claim any or all of the livestock premiums (beef special premium, suckler cow premium, sheep annual premium and hill livestock compensatory allowance).[7] Those animal aid applications have to be submitted in accordance with the detailed rules relating to those schemes.[8]

Member States can decide that a single application can cover several animal aid applications and an area aid application can be combined with one or more animal aid applications.[9]

The UK has opted for a single IACS application covering animal and area aid. Applications for specific livestock aids in accordance with those schemes will be made separately. Whether it is an area aid application or an animal aid application the integrated control system covers it.[10] Thus it is subject to administrative checks, on-the-spot checks and, if appropriate, verification by ariel or satellite remote sensing.[11]

It is appropriate to consider the IACS requirements in relation to the two forms of aid application (area aid application and livestock aid application) regardless of any additional requirements imposed under the specific schemes.[12]

(a) Area aid applications

Area aid applications have to contain "all necessary information".[13]

---

1 Article 6.3 of Council Regulation 3508/92.
2 Article 6.4 of Council Regulation 3508/92.
3 Article 6.1 of Council Regulation 3508/92.
4 Article 6.6 of Council Regulation 3508/92.
· 5 Article 6.9 of Council Regulation 3508/92.
6 Article 6.7 of Council Regulation 3508/92.
7 Article 6.8 of Council Regulation 3508/92 and Article 42 of Commission Regulation 3886/92.
8 Article 6.8 of Council Regulation 3508/92.
9 Article 6.10 of Council Regulation 3508/92.
10 Article 7 of Council Regulation 3508/92.
11 Article 7 of Council Regulation 3508/92.
12 See for example Article 24 of Commission Regulation 3886/92 in relation to suckler cow premium.
13 Article 4.1 of Commission Regulation 3887/92.

Included are:

- the identity of the farmer
- particulars permitting identification of all parcels on the holding
- the area and location of all parcels
- the use of all parcels (meaning the type of crop or ground cover or absence of a crop)
- a statement by the farmer that he is aware of the requirements pertaining to the aids in question.[1]

After the time-limit for its submission[2] the application can only be amended in cases of obvious error or with documented changes in circumstances, such as death or sale/purchase or new tenancy of holdings or when permitted by another Regulation.[3] It is not permitted to add parcels as set-aside or forage areas except in very limited circumstances and where that/those parcels have already been accounted for as set-aside land or forage areas in another farmer's application which must then be corrected.[4]

Changes of use or aid scheme are permitted except that a parcel cannot be added to set-aside for the obvious reason that it would be impossible to check compliance.[5] An area aid application can be made up to the time-limit for submitting an area aid applications for land where a crop outside the arable scheme is replaced by one within it.[6]

If an area aid application relates only to permanent pasture then there is provision which allows Member States to extend the time-limit up to the date of the first livestock aid application provided that this is no later than July 1. It is not anticipated that MAFF will avail themselves of this option.

Set-aside declarations and crop declarations under the non-food product crop scheme[7] have to be made with the area aid application or be part of it.[8]

An area aid application is not required if the farmer is only applying for:[9]

- the beef special premium/suckler cow premium and he is exempted from the stocking rate requirement and is not applying for the supplement for extensification
- the deseasonalisation premium[10]
- the ewe or she goat premium.

---

1 Article 4.1 of Commission Regulation 3887/92.
2 See Article 6.2 of Council Regulation 3508/92.
3 Article 4.2(a) of Commission Regulation 3887/92.
4 Article 4.2(a) of Commission Regulation 3887/92.
5 Article 4.2(b) of Commission Regulation 3887/92.
6 Article 4.2(c) of Commission Regulation 3887/92.
7 Article 4.3 of Commission Regulation 3887/92 and Commission Regulation 334/93.
8 Article 4.4 of Commission Regulation 3887/92.
9 Article 4.5 of Commission Regulation 3887/92.
10 Only applicable in Northern Ireland due to the autumn peak.

A central purpose of the area aid application is determination of the stocking density for livestock premiums. Thus a sound grasp of what counts as forage area is essential.

Forage crops and forage areas are defined in Regulations relating to specific regimes[1] and will include land involved in grazing agreements.[2] Thus all grazing agreements should be specified in the application provided that they comply with the definition of a forage area which has to be generally available for rearing animals (either by grazing or taking forage crops from it) for a minimum period of seven months starting on a date sometime between January 1 and March 31.[3] In addition the land has to be available to the individual farmer for rearing animals for at least four of those seven months. Also the land must genuinely form part of the producer's holding for practical farming purposes.

Since occupation only has to be for four months by the individual producer there is the possibility that within the seven-month period starting between January 1 and March 31 more than one person will use the forage area. One piece of land can only count towards one producer's forage area. If the land is being given up before the end of the seven months period it has to remain a forage area for the remainder of the period. Thus for short-term grazing agreements that will be important for the purchaser of the forage area to establish the seven-month period involved and to ensure that no other use is made of the land which might prejudice his entitlement to count the land as part of his forage area.

When a farmer who is a member of a sheep producer group applies in 1993 for sheep annual premium as well as beef special premium, suckler cow premium or arable area payments he has to include in the IACS form details of all the areas used by the group.[4] The forage area available to the sheep producer group is then assigned to the individual producers in proportion to their individual quotas, valid on January 1 1993.[5]

Commons grazing is bound to lead to a large number of complications and the only guidance to date is that it has to be assigned between individual farmers in proportion to their use or right of use of it.[6]

(b)   Livestock aid applications

As with the area aid application the livestock aid application has to contain "all necessary information" and the requirements set out below are simply the minimum IACS requirements. Those imposed under the particular schemes are dealt with in the sections dealing with each

---

1   In relation to beef special premium and suckler cow premium see Article 4g(3) of Council Regulation 805/68 as amended by Council Regulation 2066/92 and para 11.2.4(c) above.
2   See section 2 of the Agricultural Holdings Act 1986.
3   Article 2.1(c) of Commission Regulation 3887/92.
4   Article 4.6 of Commission Regulation 3887/92.
5   Article 4.6 of Commission Regulation 3887/92 and as specified in Article 5(a) of Council Regulation 3013/89.
6   Article 2.1(b) of Commission Regulation 3887/92 and see para 6 of Annex 1 of MAAF Explanatory Booklet.

scheme. The application has to include:[1]

- the identification of the farmer
- reference to the area aid application submitted
- the number of animals of each species in respect of which any aid is applied for
- where applicable, an undertaking by the applicant to comply with retention periods
- the location of the animals
- the identification numbers of the animals
- the quotas for the animals concerned
- the farmers milk quota
- a statement by the farmer that he is aware of the requirements pertaining to the aid in question.

Applications for HLCAs have to be lodged by a date determined by Member States.[2]

20.3.5   The integrated control system
The integrated control system covers all aid applications submitted and involves

- administrative checks and
- on-the-spot checks and
- if appropriate verification by aerial or satellite remote sensing.[3]

Member States or designated authorities in Member States have to carry out administrative and on the spot checks and may do remote sensing.[4] The purpose of administrative and on-the-spot checks is to ensure effective compliance with aid and premium rules. This monitoring system includes cross-checks on parcels and animals to ensure that neither is claimed for twice in one year.[5]

On the spot checks have to cover a minimum of 10% of livestock aid applications and 5% of area aid applications.[6] Significant irregularities will increase these percentages.[7] In selecting which producers to subject to on the spot checks the inspecting authority has to bear in mind risk analysis and representativeness.[8] Risk analysis takes account of, *inter alia*,

- the amount of aid involved
- the number of parcels and the area or number of animals for which aid is requested

---

1   Article 5.1 of Commission Regulation 3887/92.
2   Article 5.2 of Commission Regulation 3887/92.
3   Article 7 of Council Regulation 3508/92.
4   Article 8 of Council Regulation 3508/92.
5   Article 6.2 of Commission Regulation 3387/92.
6   Article 6.3 of Commission Regulation 3887/92.
7   Article 6.3 of Commission Regulation 3887/92.
8   Article 6.4 of Commission Regulation 3887/92.

- changes from the previous year
- the findings of checks made in past years
- other factors to be defined by the Member State.

Essentially on the spot checks should be unannounced but up to 48 hours notice may be given.[1] At least 50% of the checks on livestock have to be carried out in the relevant retention period.[2]

Every inspection visit has to be fully documented setting out:

- the reasons for the visit
- the persons present
- the number of parcels visited
- those measured
- the measuring methods used
- the number of animals of each species found
- where applicable their identity numbers.[3]

Inspections under the old regimes have taken place but from the above list it is plain that non-compliance would be hard to disguise in the event of a thorough check taking place. Farmers or their agents will have the opportunity to sign the inspection report so that they must presumably be given a chance to read the report and they will have the opportunity to add their own comments.[4]

Probably the worst move the farmer can make is to refuse an on-the-spot inspection. This results in automatic rejection of his aid application unless he can demonstrate force majeure.[5]

The sizes of parcels are to be checked by reference to officially acceptable published material.[6] In the UK MAFF requires[7] that producers use ordnance survey maps or other professionally drawn maps on a scale of at least 1:10,000 (larger scale will be accepted) and these must show clearly

- the OS sheet number, scale and copyright date
- the national grid lines
- the boundaries of any land farmed
- any permanent field boundaries or other changes to the land farmed since the map was printed
- the OS field size for each field farmed in hectares rounded to two decimal places
- the four-figure national grid field number for each field farmed; and
- all existing vernacular buildings, stone walls, hedges, rows of trees (including hedgerow trees), watercourses, ditches, ponds, pools, lochs,

---

1 Article 6.5 of Commission Regulation 3887/92.
2 Second Paragraph of Article 6.5 of Commission Regulation 3887/92.
3 Article 12 of Commission Regulation 3887/92.
4 Article 12 of Commission Regulation 3887/92.
5 Article 13 of Commission Regulation 3887/92.
6 Article 6.7 of Commission Regulation 3887/92.
7 See MAFF Press Release 77/93 of March 8 1993.

lakes which are entitled to be maintained and which are situated on, or adjacent to, land that is eligible for arable area payments.

It will be permissible for farmers to write in required information which is not already included on existing maps.

No tolerance margin has yet been set by MAFF but a major improvement on the confusion caused previously under the oil seeds regime is that the total area of the parcel can be claimed for if it is fully utilised accordingly to local standards.[1] Therefore no deductions for field margins will be required but other features within the field will have to be deducted (roads, buildings, footpaths and ponds for example).

The provision of maps is obligatory for those applying for arable area aids, and although technically not required for those only applying for forage area, the detail required on the form includes field numbers and map references, so that maps must be available, even if not sent in. The requirement for maps will prove a major headache for farmers and their advisors in submitting applications by the May 15 1993 deadline. Some parts of the United Kingdom are not covered by the 1:2,500 series of Ordnance Survey maps, which is the only series containing the detail required in terms of field parcel numbers and hectares. In many other areas where these maps are available, many of the fields are missing this information.

20.4   Penalties

There are draconian penalties for late lodgement of aid applications.[2] The necessity for a time-limit is to prevent fraud and doubtless careful consideration was given to the question of proportionality.[3] On many occasions in similar circumstances similarly draconian penalties have been upheld by the European Court.

20.4.1   Late applications

For every working day that an application, whether for area aid or livestock aid, is late a 1% reduction is applied to the amount of entitlement under the application up to a maximum of 20 days. After 20 days delay the application is inadmissible and no aid is paid.[4] This would apply equally to any entitlement to livestock premium which depended upon the IACS declaration of forage area. This rule applies to amendments to area aid applications[5] and advanced payments for oil seeds.

The only exception is in case of force majeure.

20.4.2   Inaccurate applications

The penalties for inaccuracies in both the area aid application and

---

1   Article 6.7 of Commission Regulation 3887/92.
2   See Article 8 of Commission Regulation 3887/92.
3   See Ninth Recital to Commission Regulation 3887/92.
4   Article 8.1 of Commission Regulation 3887/92.
5   See Article 4.2(a) of Commission Regulation 3887/92.

livestock application fall into three categories:

(i)   under declaration
(ii) over declaration
(iii) intentionally false or seriously negligent

and are graduated accordingly.

(a)   Arable applications

Under declaration is where the area actually determined is greater than the area aid application. Only the area claimed for in the application is compensated.[1] If there is over declaration then the area determined on inspection is used if the over declaration is of less than 2%. If it is between 2% and 10% then twice the difference will be deducted. If it is between 10% and 20% the reduction is 30% and if the over declaration exceeds 20% no area linked aid at all is paid.

The only exception is force majeure unless the error in area determination came from a source recognised by the competent authority.[2]

Intentionally false or seriously negligent over declarations lead to exclusion from payment from the aid scheme concerned for the year in question and intentionally false declarations lead to exclusion from the arable aid scheme in the following year for an area equal to that for which the aid application was rejected.[3]

Furthermore, it should be noted that any breach by a farmer of his obligations under the non-food set-aside scheme results in the farmer being treated as if the set-aside parcels had not been found on inspection. Depending upon the acreage involved this might have a drastic effect on the farm business with its concomitant loss of set-aside leading to loss of area compensatory payments.

Forage areas, set-aside areas and each arable crop area for which a different aid rate is applicable (in 1993 different rates were applicable to cereals, oil seeds, proteins and set-aside) are treated separately[4] so that a seriously negligent over declaration in oil seeds excludes a producer from aid for oil seed in that year but not for cereals and proteins.

Whatever area is determined as being the correct area of the application, it is this figure that is used where set-aside is involved for calculating the maximum compensatory payments for arable crops under the general scheme and for calculating stocking density and extensification premium in claims for suckler cow premium and beef special premium.[5] As long as the over declaration does not exceed 20%

---

1   Article 9.1 of Commission Regulation 3887/92. MAFF's view is that these provisions apply when the declared area does not equal the actual area because of an incorrect statement of area or because the rules of the scheme have been infringed. Contrast with Article 5 of Commission Regulation 2293/92.
2   Article 9.2 of Commission Regulation 3887/92.
3   Article 9.2 of Commission Regulation 3887/92.
4   Article 9.3 of Commission Regulation 3887/92.
5   Article 9.4 of Commission Regulation 3887/92.

the arable compensatory payment is made on the basis of the area of set-aside actually determined.

Rape seed of the wrong variety or quality is not eligible for any aid.[1]

(b)   Livestock applications

Aid will not be paid for claims exceeding a producer's sheep annual premium or suckler cow premium quota.[2] If animal numbers are under-declared the producer is limited to the number in the application.[3] If the number of animals claimed for exceeds the animals found on inspection then aid is calculated by reference to the animals found.

However, except in cases of force majeure aid is reduced

(a) if the application is in respect of 20 animals or less by:
   (i)   the percentage of the difference found if this is less than two animals
   (ii) twice the percentage if the difference is more than two animals but less than four
   (iii) one hundred percent if the difference is greater than four animals
   based on the numbers declared.
(b) If the application is in respect of more than 20 animals aid will be reduced by:
   (i)   the percentage corresponding to the difference if less than 5%
   (ii) by 20% if the difference is between 5% and 10%
   (iii) by 40% if the difference is greater than 10% but less than 20%
   (iv) by 100% if the difference is greater than 20%

based on the numbers found.[4]

In the case of false or seriously negligent claims the farmer is excluded from the aid scheme concerned for that year and if intentionally false he is excluded from the same aid scheme for the following year.[5]

If force majeure results in a farmer being unable to comply with his retention undertaking the right to premium is retained in respect of the number of animals eligible at the time of the force majeure.[6]

There is an additional barrage of complex penalty arrangements for when on-farm checks reveal that prior to application there are fewer animals on the farm than are likely to be claimed for. Except in cases of force majeure "the total amount of the special premiums shall be reduced proportionately". Exactly what the proportionate reduction is is not clear but it might be the proportion between the number of animals likely to be claimed for compared with the number of animals actually on the holding.[7]

---

1   Article 9.5 of Commission Regulation 3887/92.
2   Article 10.1 of Commission Regulation 3887/92.
3   Article 10.2 of Commission Regulation 3887/92.
4   Article 10.2 of Commission Regulation 3887/92.
5   Article 10.2 of Commission Regulation 3887/92.
6   Article 10.2 of Commission Regulation 3887/92.
7   Article 10.3 of Commission Regulation 3887/92.

If the farm's stock record book compared with the numbers of animals present shows a difference of 20% or more or if a 3% or two animal inaccuracy is found on two checks in the same year, no premium is granted for that year.[1] If the inaccuracies in the farm stock record book are found to be intentional or due to serious neglect the applicant is excluded from the special premium scheme for that year and the next.

Male bovine animals present on a producers holding are not included unless they are identified in the application or when on-farm checks take place prior to application in the farm stock record book.[2] Individual identification is not necessary for suckler cows declared for suckler cow premiums nor for bovines declared for HLCAs. These may be replaced by another suckler cow or bovine respectively provided that replacement occurs on farm within 20 days and is entered in the farm stock register within three days thereafter.[3]

Where a farmer finds "owing to the impact of natural circumstances" (presumably this will most often be death) that he cannot keep all his animals for the retention period he can claim for the numbers actually kept throughout the period so long as he notifies the competent authority within 10 days of finding any reduction in animal numbers.[4]

All of the penalties in the integrated system are without prejudice to additional penalties provided for by Member States.[5]

20.5   Force majeure

Over the forthcoming years there are going to be many farmers and their advisers who turn anxiously to Article 11 of Commission Regulation 3887/92 to ascertain whether they can avail themselves of the force majeure exception. Inevitably most of these people will be those who have made innocent mistakes. Instead of comfort they are likely to find at worst disappointment and at best a hard road ahead. The circumstances in which force majeure can apply and in which an exception to the penalties provisions can be found are likely to be very limited.

First, a case of force majeure has to be reported to the competent authority within 10 days of the date when the farmer is in a position to do so.[6] Delay is likely to be a problem since if something catastrophic happens attention is naturally diverted to trying to deal with the problem rather than reporting it. There is no power to extend time but there is some flexibility in determining the date on which the farmer was first in a position to report. If this is implemented with a measure of common sense the time-period should not commence running until at least the initial upheaval resulting from natural disaster, accidents and illness has been overcome.

---

1 Article 10.3 of Commission Regulation 3887/92.
2 Article 10.4 of Commission Regulation 3887/92
3 Article 10.4 of Commission Regulation 3887/92.
4 Article 10.5 of Commission Regulation 3887/92.
5 See for example Regulation 10 of the Hill Livestock (Compensatory Allowances) Regulations 1992 and SI 1992 No. 269.
6 Article 11.1 of Commission Regulation 3887/92.

There can never be an exhaustive list of circumstances which constitute force majeure but the competent authorities are permitted to recognise at least the following as force majeure:

(a) the death of the farmer
(b) long-term professional incapacity of the farmer
(c) expropriation of a major part of the agricultural land managed by the farmer if such expropriation could not be anticipated on the day the application was lodged
(d) a severe natural disaster gravely affecting the holding's agricultural land
(e) the accidental destruction of livestock buildings on the holding
(f) an epizootic affecting part or all of the farmer's livestock.

It will be noted that the only expressed case that might assist a farmer making an honest error in vaguely normal circumstances is long-term professional incapacity. Experience in other regimes suggest that this is going to be very difficult and will require that there are unusual circumstances, outside the control of the farmer, the consequences of which, in spite of the exercise of all due care, could not have been avoided except at the cost of excessive sacrifice.

It is commonly believed that force majeure is in itself a general principle of community law and in certain circumstances the Court of Justice has accepted the principle of force majeure.[1] However the Commission refuses to accept force majeure as a general principle of law in itself but accepts that much the same result is achieved by viewing it as an aspect of the accepted principle of proportionality.[2] If this is right, the force majeure provisions in the penalties of the IACS system have to be viewed as part of the wider consideration of whether the penalties are proportional.

The Commission's view is that force majeure comprises both an objective element and a subjective element. The Commission's view is that the objective element must amount to unusual circumstances outside the control of the trader involved and that the subjective element must involve consequences which would not have been avoided in spite of the exercisable due care. With regard to the objective element the Commission state that

> It is important to establish the definition of an unusual circumstance which is outside the control of the trader. The court has not as yet been required to give a very precise ruling nevertheless it makes a distinction between normal commercial risks (inherent in each transaction of the same type) and those which are abnormal.[3]

An abnormal circumstance is said to be one which is unforeseeable or at least so improbable that a businessman exercising all due care could

---

1 See *Reich* case (64/74) [1975] ECR 261 and *Schwarzwaldmilch* case (4/68) [1968] ECR 377.
2 Commission Notice C(88) 1696.
3 See Case 38/79 *Nordmark* [1980] ECR 643.

consider the risk to be negligible. Examples are given of things the risk of which are considered negligible and the examples given are a stroke of lightening, ice-bound waterways and an avalanche blocking roads which are normally open in winter. To be an abnormal circumstance it has to be outside the control of the trader in the broad sense of being a natural disaster or a sovereign act or a wild cat strike. The Commission's view is that acts are not outside a trader's control, even if fraudulent, if they are committed by those with whom a trader has contractual relations since it is the trader's responsibility to select his trading partners with care and to place them under an obligation in the contract in a way which is sufficiently binding on them to comply with the terms of the contract (where appropriate by making provision for penalties in the event of a failure to fulfil contractual obligations). This would appear to be a very onerous and rather unrealistic approach although not wholly unsupported by authority.[1]

A subjective element apparently entails the obligation to guard against the consequences of the abnormal occurrence by taking more appropriate measures unless they involve an excessive sacrifice. In particular it is that the trader has to carefully monitor the progress of what he is doing and take action without delay if he detects any anomaly or where appropriate has to obtain supplies elsewhere or deal with goods in another way. In short he has to mitigate his loss and must protect himself in an appropriate manner from the loss of important documents and exercise all due care in order to comply with the time-limit prescribed in the rules.

Unfortunately it must be probable that it is going to be only very rarely that traders will be able to establish that they have not complied with the time-limit in the context of the CAP without having failed to exercise all due care.

It should also be noted that the burden of proof lies on anyone trying to prove force majeure and the Commission hope to see incontrovertible documentary evidence to support a claim although they do concede that that may not always be possible in all circumstances.

The principle of proportionality requires that the means used by the authorities must be in proportion to their purpose. In the leading case[2] the Court of Justice held:

> In exercising their powers, the Institutions must ensure that the amounts which commercial operators are charged are no greater than is required to achieve the aim which the authorities are to accomplish; however, it does not necessarily follow that that obligation must be measured to the individual situation with any one particular group of operators.
>
> Given the multiplicity and complexity of economic circumstances, such an evaluation would not only be impossible to achieve but would also create perpetual uncertainty in the law.
>
> An overall assessment of the advantages and disadvantages of the measures contemplated was justified, in this case, by the exceptionally need for

---

1 Case 42/79 *Eierkontor* [1979] ECR 3703.
2 Second *Schluter* case (9/72) [1973] ECR 1156.

practicability in economic measures which are designed to exert an immediate corrective influence; and this need had to be taken into account in balancing the opposing interests.

Thus when viewing the proportionality of a provision one examines whether the means employed to achieve its aim correspond to the importance of the aim and whether the means were necessary for its achievement. With the imposition of penalties the sanction must be appropriate and necessary to achieve the purpose of the Regulation. It is highly relevant to look at the matter from the point of view of the authority seeking to impose the penalty to see what alternatives were open to it and to investigate the difficulties that it would be placed in but for the sanction. The grading of the penalties according to the size and severity of the breaches as set out in the IACS system is an indication of the intention to observe the principle of proportionality.

Member States are obliged to notify the Commission of cases which they recognise as force majeure.[1] Historically, in relation to other regimes some Member States find it easier to identify force majeure and then fail to notify the Commission than others.

20.6   Wrong payments

Wrong payment means overpayment to the farmer. When this is detected the farmer has to repay the excess together with interest thereon from the date when he received the money to the date when he repays it.[2] The rate of interest is left for determination under national law but if the overpayment was the fault of the competent authority and not the fault of the farmer either no interest at all is payable or at the most an amount which represents undue profit made by the farmer.[3] It remains to be seen whether the UK authorities will argue that undue profit has been made where a farmer has merely reduced his bank overdraft. Equally fascinating is what meaning the word "undue" will be given. Since by definition none of the overpayment was due then all interest earned or interest charges saved could be said to be "undue" profit but if the word is to have real meaning perhaps it should be restricted to excessive profit? Unfortunately for farmers Member States can deduct any overpayments from the first advance or first payment due to the farmer concerned after the date when the decision to seek repayment is taken. Interest ceases running when the farmer is told of the overpayment in these circumstances.[4] The rules allow for flexibility in the decision not to recover small amounts of overpayments (20 ECUs or less).[5]

---

1   Article 11.3 of Commission Regulation 3887/92.
2   Article 14.1 of Commission Regulation 3887/92.
3   Third paragraph of Article 14.1 of Commission Regulation 3887/92.
4   Article 14.2 of Commission Regulation 3887/92.
5   Article 14.3 of Commission Regulation 3887/92.

20.7   Minimum size of application

The minimum size of an application is 50 ECUs.[1] The minimum size of an agricultural parcel in respect of which area aid can be claimed is 0.3 ha unless Member States specify a smaller minimum size. The UK is proposing to utilise a minimum size of 0.1 ha for any parcel provided that the total claim exceeds 0.3 ha. In certain circumstances 0.01 ha (seed plots etc) will be allowed.

20.8   Role of commission officials

The role of commission officials is strictly limited in the field of checks and verification. Commission officials are expressly forbidden from participating in home visits or formal interrogation of suspects made under the criminal law albeit they are allowed access to information obtained by such means.[2] Whether this means that UK farmers can expect commission officials to turn up at farm offices and carry out informal interrogations remains to be seen.

20.9   Expense

Member States are eligible to receive a contribution from the Community towards the considerable cost of setting up the computerised and checking structures as well as carrying out remote sensing.[3] The total expenditure is shared among Member States and the UK's share is 9.9% subject to a ceiling of not more than 50% of the payments made in a year.[4]

20.10   Implementation in the UK

Member states are obliged to implement the integrated system in full by January 1 1996 and from February 1 1993 the aid applications and integrated control system as well as the alphanumeric system of identification and registration of bovine animals applies.[5]

In the UK the operative parts of IACS apply to arable area payments, beef special premium and suckler cow premium for 1993.

Thus, for 1993 at least, IACS will not involve the computerised data base nor does it cover the sheep regime or HLCAs.[6]

Although the initial area aid application to land on farmers' desks in 1993 does not cover sheep annual premium and hill livestock compensatory allowances, there is one aspect that should be much simpler for most farmers in 1994. This is the Doomsday aspect or

---

1 Article 2.4 of Commission Regulation 3887/92.
2 Article 11.2 of Council Regulation 3508/92.
3 Article 7 of Commission Regulation 3887/92.
4 Article 10 of Council Regulation 3508/92 and Annex to Commission Regulation 3887/92.
5 Article 13 of Council Regulation 3508/92.
6 Article 19 of Commission Regulation 3887/92.

registration of eligible land, together with the provision of detailed maps (obligatory for all wishing to claim arable area payments or to register land for possible future arable claims). The registration of land will all be fed into a computer database and, providing there are no changes, this should make application in future years much simpler.

The basic information required by IACS is the same right through the 12 countries in Europe, but the actual forms sent out will vary considerably. This is even the case within the United Kingdom with MAFF in England and Wales taking a different approach from the Scottish Office. The package sent out by MAFF contains the following:

IACS I – Explanatory booklet (79 pages)
IACS II – Arable area application: base form
IACS IIa – Field data sheet
IACS III – Example map and field data sheet

The package sent out by the Scottish Office consists of the following:

IACS I – Explanatory booklet on Integrated Administration and Control System (13 pages)
IACS II – Area aid application
IACS III – Explanatory notes to assist completion of area aid application (11 pages)

Within these different approaches the basic information required is listed below:

* Basic business information (name, address, etc)
* Basic field information (field number, hectares, OS sheet number, land use at December 31 1991)
* Forage area (fields, hectares, crop, availability, shared grazing and common land)
* Arable area applications (cereals, oilseeds, protein and set-aside both fallow and non-food crop)
* Other land (other crops being grown in 1993)

G. A FINAL THOUGHT

A final thought

21   The fact that it can have been necessary to write a book of this length and complexity coupled with the cost to the taxpayers of the Community of administering the new system of aid for farmers may in themselves be indictments of the entire system.

Could the way ahead lie in the German route[1] of paying farmers part of their income in straightforward area aid for every utilised hectare of agricultural land without any link to prices or production?
The administration costs would be minimal and the scope for fraud would be minimal.

Alternatively a system could be based on business turnover or on standard gross margins (a concept already adopted in Europe). If the present reforms pave the way towards a move to world prices, and if as a result world prices increase so as to improve returns from the market, then compensation payments could eventually be phased out and the CAP reforms would just about become defensible. Would our protected and some would say cossetted European farmers be prepared to face up to such financial reality? Perhaps they will be after living with the burgeoning bureaucracy for a few years.

---

1   93/C 97/08 COM (93) 94 Final.

Index

References in the main text are to paragraph number